# COOK FOR TOMORROW

# Cook for Tomorrow

## Anne Mason

# THE COOKERY BOOK CLUB

THIS EDITION PUBLISHED BY
THE COOKERY BOOK CLUB 1969
BY ARRANGEMENT WITH
ANDRE DEUTSCH LIMITED

PRINTED IN GREAT BRITAIN
BY EBENEZER BAYLIS AND SON LTD
THE TRINITY PRESS, WORCESTER, AND LONDON

# Contents

# Introduction

A woman who is expected to do the major jobs of cooking and housekeeping, as well as doing a job outside the home, must plan her time very carefully, and this book has been written primarily to help the many thousands of women who work away from home but who still like to cook well for the enjoyment of their family or friends. And I hope that full-time housewives, whose days are so much fuller than envious career women suspect, and whose husbands are just as likely to bring home unexpected guests, will also find it useful.

As a busy journalist who has carried out the job of housekeeping for my family for quite a long time, I have learned by trial and error the importance of careful planning, particularly where meals are concerned. The recipes and suggestions given here have saved me many an exhausting scramble.

In the majority of recipes the major part of preparation and cooking is done the night before, and the dish needs only re-heating and garnishing before serving. I have tried to keep this second stage to within thirty minutes, which is a reasonable time to allow for cooking and serving a dinner.

In a few cases preparations must be done in the morning before leaving home, but none of these are very difficult or time-consuming, and they can be carried out while you watch the toast for breakfast.

To borrow the motto of the Boy Scouts, every housewife-career woman should 'Be Prepared' when planning and cooking meals.

## PLAN TO SAVE TIME

Learn to plan ahead in your shopping, in the meals you will be serving, and in your essential household chores. Keep a large slate or blackboard on the kitchen wall as a memory aid. Here you can write down your time schedules for cooking, and your shopping list for each day.

Learn to distinguish between the essential jobs, and those which can be put off for a few days if necessary. Perhaps those unwashed windows worry you, but you haven't time to wash them this week-end because young John is having some boys home for supper. Concentrate on making his favourite dishes and forget the windows for the time. They will still be there next week, but his pleasure in being able to entertain his friends is much more important today.

Look around your kitchen carefully and see if it can be re-arranged more conveniently than it is at present.

A place for everything and everything in its right place is a good rule for anybody, but especially for a woman who comes home in a hurry to cook the dinner and wants to be able to put her hand on the necessary knives, cooking spoons, saucepans or strainers almost without looking for them. Taking out and putting away should be almost automatic.

Personally, I like to have much-used equipment hanging up within reach of my hand as I stand at my kitchen work-bench, rather than having to reach into a cupboard for it. Today's kitchen utensils and small equipment are well-made and can be bought in sets with matching coloured handles, which give a decorative look to the kitchen wall. Useful racks and shelves which are easily fixed on the wall help to keep these gadgets tidy.

Above my work-bench I have two racks and a shelf, all in bright red plastic which only needs a wipe-over to clean. On the shelf are screw-top jars containing garlic, bay leaves, peppercorns and mixed herbs, all seasonings I use frequently and want within reach. Salt and pepper containers are kept

8

beside the stove where they are most often used. Hanging from the racks are my most-used gadgets, such as kitchen scissors, a perforated spoon, a flexible spatula, an egg slice, a soup ladle (good for dishing stews as well as soups), a small aluminium strainer for vegetables and, in the summer, a plastic salad basket for lettuce.

These are the things I like to have on hand when I am cooking. You will probably find there are other things you need for your convenience, as everybody's needs are different when they are cooking the dishes they like.

## EQUIPPING YOUR KITCHEN

A good workman must have good tools to work with, and this is just as true for a woman who is 'chief cook and bottle washer' in her spare time. The right knife can make preparing a grapefruit so much easier and quicker; a casserole of the proper size gives a more satisfactory dish; and an electric beater makes the job of whipping cream or preparing a cake-batter more economical in time and trouble.

Even if you cannot have everything from a dish-washing machine to an automatic cooker all at once, there are many quite inexpensive kitchen tools you can buy one at a time to make your cooking preparations easier, and on the following pages you will find a list of useful things for the woman who thinks cooking well is worthwhile. Many of them you probably have already if you have been a housewife for some time, but such a list will be useful for those setting up house for the first time – whether as a newly-married or as a new business woman living away from home:

set of good quality saucepans     colander
frying pan     fine wire strainers
deep-fat frying pan with     (1 large, 1 small)
    basket     flan tin, pie plate, pie dish
double saucepan     cake tins, assorted sizes
omelette pan     (1 with removable base)

9

pastry board and rolling pin
pastry cutters, plain and fluted
pastry brush, flour dredger
baking trays
roasting pan
set of long skewers for kebabs
good corkscrew
grater and shredder (plastic)
lemon squeezer
wall can-opener
2 wire whisks (large and small)
salt box
plastic containers for refrigerator
plastic bags in assorted sizes
casseroles, assorted sizes (ovenproof glass or earthenware)
small individual ramekins

mixing bowls, assorted sizes
jelly moulds
plastic salad shaker (for lettuce)
quart measuring jug
standard cup measure
kitchen scales
thick chopping board
pepper grinder
set of sharp kitchen knives
curved grapefruit knife
knife-sharpener
scissors
flexible stainless spatula
cooking forks and spoons
wooden spoons
perforated spoon
aluminium strainer
soup ladle
egg slice
aluminium cooking foil

Larger pieces of equipment to make cooking jobs easier depend on the requirements of the family, and the kind of food they like to eat.

Another factor which is important when choosing such equipment is whether you like to entertain your friends for meals, and give frequent dinner parties.

Among the equipment I consider essential to enable me to produce meals in quick time for both my family and our frequent dinner guests are an electric beater and an electric blender, both of which are invaluable for many kinds of jobs. You can beat up a cake, make mayonnaise or whip cream so much quicker and with so much less trouble with an electric beater. A blender will make purées, convert milk and ice cream into a milk-shake for a thirsty youngster, or crush breadcrumbs in a matter of seconds. Neither of these articles is very expensive, and the beater hangs on the wall ready to hand when I need it.

My electric Foldaway spit-roaster is not absolutely essential, but it is a great boon with its large grilling space and quick but easily controlled heat. With the rotating kebab attachment and long skewers I can use up all kinds of meat and vegetables to make tasty meals which my family and friends know as 'dining off a dagger' (the recipes for many of which you will find on pages 109–12).

The spit-roaster (it is also obtainable for gas) being reasonably portable, is also useful for buffet parties, when guests can make up their own kebabs and watch them grilling. During week-ends I can fix two good-sized chickens on the rotating spit and leave them to cook for dinner while I get on with something else, just taking an occasional look to see they are all right without having to bend down to open the oven. Cooking two at once gives me chicken for another meal later in the week.

If you are buying a new stove, investigate the automatic cooker, either gas or electric. With one of these you can set the clock at the time you want it to start cooking, and also the time to switch off. You can put a prepared casserole in the oven, with vegetables in another casserole, and a pudding on the next shelf, and come home to a well-cooked meal ready at the time you want it.

If you already have a modern electric cooker, you can probably have an automatic timer fitted to it without much trouble or expense, but this is not possible with existing gas cookers, only those you buy new and completely equipped.

A pressure cooker is another aid to the busy cook, and for those who can afford one a home-freezer is a great boon. I need not stress the importance of a refrigerator, which is almost as essential as your oven. Buy the biggest 'fridge you can afford or have space for, and learn how to make the best use of it.

## USE YOUR REFRIGERATOR WISELY

Ideally, your refrigerator should be placed in the main work-area of the kitchen – that is, near the sink and work-bench, if the shape of your kitchen permits.

Never overload the refrigerator. If it is to work efficiently it must have adequate air-circulation inside, and foods packed too tightly together will not get the even cold which is necessary to keep them in good condition.

Don't buy frozen foods in the morning and expect them to remain frozen until you get home to store them in the freezing compartment of the refrigerator. Once food has thawed to any degree it should never be re-frozen, but should be eaten within twenty-four hours.

If yours is not an automatic defrosting model, you will need to defrost the refrigerator regularly to get rid of excess frosting or icing which slows up the efficiency of the machine. This is the best time to clean out the cabinet, and get rid of any bits and pieces you haven't had time to use up. If you have been careful to wipe up any spills as they happen, the cabinet should need only a wipe over with a cloth wrung out in warm water to which you have added a teaspoon of bicarbonate of soda to each pint of water used.

When you go away on holiday and leave the house unoccupied, empty the refrigerator, defrost it and wipe clean both inside and outside, then leave the door open to prevent it becoming musty.

Always wrap or cover foods before they go into the 'fridge, but do not leave the meat in its butcher's paper. Use polythene, aluminium cooking foil, or plastic bags for wrapping; make use of screw-top jars for sauces and other liquids, or the special plastic boxes and bowls with tight-fitting lids which are made especially for refrigerator use. These help to keep foods fresh, and prevent drying out of natural juices and loss of flavour. They also prevent your cabinet from becoming a chaos of conflicting flavours and smells.

Keep the caps on milk and cream bottles. Store butter in its original wrapping in the section specially designed for butter. Cheese keeps well in the 'fridge, but wrap it in greaseproof paper or foil and bring to room temperature before serving.

Unwrap fresh meat or poultry when you get it home, and if not using at once, place in a plastic bag, seal firmly and store in the part of the refrigerator nearest to the ice-making compartment. Frozen meat or poultry in special packs should be stored in its original wrap. Uncooked meat or poultry should keep up to four days in the coldest part of the 'fridge, but do not keep minced meat more than two days.

I never like to keep fresh fish longer than overnight in the 'fridge, and it should be wrapped in foil or a plastic bag before storing nearest the ice-making compartment. If you have a large freezing compartment, fish should be quite safe there for two days, and of course, unthawed frozen packaged fish will keep for four or five days in the freezing section.

Vegetables you have prepared overnight for cooking next day should be stored in plastic bags or covered containers. Pastry can be made the night before; pancake batters can be mixed and stored in a covered basin or jug; eggs can be hard-boiled. All these can be left in the refrigerator ready for cooking when you get home.

Food cooked in casseroles can be left in them, covered and put into the refrigerator, but they should be completely cooled before storing. This last applies to all cooked foods, which should always be cooled before putting into the refrigerator.

But remember that ovenproof dishes or casseroles that have been left in the 'fridge *must* be brought back to room temperature before re-heating in the oven, or there is the risk of cracking or breaking. Standing the uncovered casserole in a container of warm (not hot) water speeds up this process if you are in a hurry.

## PLANNING A DINNER PARTY

Planning a meal as a way of entertaining friends calls for careful organization when you are away from home all day, and the meal must be one which can be cooked and served in a limited time.

There are many recipes in this book which will help you cope with this problem, but the main thing is to decide what you want to serve as the main course. This can depend on the time of year and what is readily available, but there are certain rules which can help you plan your dinner once you have chosen the main dish.

Presuming a three-course dinner is to be served (and you would be wise to limit yourself to this), with Braised Beef Rolls in red wine (page 77) as the main dish, you would not serve a heavy soup to begin with, but rather something like Baked Grapefruit (page 20), which is prepared before you leave home in the morning. This means you cannot serve a fruit dessert to finish the meal, but a Meringue Torte (page 177) prepared the night before, would be ideal.

Alternatively, serve a fish hors d'oeuvre such as Crab in Cucumber Cups (page 19) to start the meal, and Strawberries Marie-Therese (page 192) or Lemon Mousse (page 181) as the dessert. When entertaining guests whose tastes you don't know, choose dishes you know you prepare well and which are popular with your family (usually your severest critics). Keep the meal simple rather than too elaborate – better to serve Minted Grilled Chops (page 94) followed by a special Brazilian Parfait (page 199) you prepared the night before, rather than attempt too many dishes in the limited time at your disposal. Simple dishes are always acceptable if well cooked, well garnished and well served.

Remember also to consider the appearance and colour of your dishes. Don't serve creamy mashed potatoes, however nice, with fish in white sauce – but if you add chopped parsley or chives to the mashed potatoes, and a sprinkle of

14

paprika to the sauce, and serve buttered carrot sticks or grilled tomato halves, you will have a colourful and appetizing meal.

The cook who is also the hostess has the best chance of serving a perfect meal if she chooses a main course which will not spoil if kept hot after the time she had planned to serve. This is where casserole dishes are so useful, as they can usually be left in a slightly lowered temperature for some time without harm. A cold first course which can be put on the table before guests arrive is also a boon, as it allows the hostess to welcome her guests knowing nothing will burn if she spends a little time with them.

If serving soup as the first course, serve it from a tureen (or use a large covered vegetable dish) at the table rather than dishing it up in the kitchen and carrying it in when guests are seated. A tureen is not only more convenient, but keeps the soup hot. Of course, this does not apply when serving cold soup, such as Vichyssoise (page 35), which can be served in small bowls and placed on the table beforehand.

Some main courses lend themselves to being served at the table, or, if more convenient, from a side table in the dining room. Unless the dessert has been made originally in individual dishes it is pleasant to serve it at the table, with cream separately for people to help themselves.

For an informal shish-kebab party, if you have a spit-roaster, assemble a number of different ingredients in bowls (marinade overnight those foods which need it) and let people assemble their own choice of foods on skewers. Cook a big pan of rice and keep it hot over boiling water, then dish it out on heated plates when the kebabs are cooked. Prepare one or two desserts the night before and let people help themselves when the kebabs are finished. Serve a basket of crisp rolls, or prepare garlic bread, and your buffet party is sure to be a success without too much trouble on your part.

Garlic bread should be prepared well beforehand, then warmed in the oven before serving. Use the long crunchy loaves of French bread and cut in 1-inch slices but without cutting through the bottom crust. Blend crushed garlic in butter and spread on the bread slices, pressing them back into the original shape. Wrap in foil and warm just before serving.

# Hors d'Oeuvre and Party Savouries

In many cases it is very difficult to say when a prepared dish ceases to be an hors d'oeuvre and becomes a party savoury, so here you will find them all in the one chapter.

From here you can take your pick as occasion demands, sometimes serving stuffed eggs or piquant crab fingers for hors d'oeuvre as the first course for dinner with friends, or at other times serving the same tasty savouries for a supper party or a buffet dinner.

Hors d'oeuvre should not be too complicated or too filling, or your guests will not be able to appreciate the dinner to follow.

I like the Italian idea of antipasti, which is the same idea as hors d'oeuvre, but much simpler. They serve slices of salami in endless varieties; delicious Parma ham; canned fish such as anchovies and tuna; freshly cooked mussels and prawns; sliced raw mushrooms; cooked green beans in an oil and vinegar dressing; and artichoke hearts. All are simple to prepare and most attractive to look at when served and arranged for colour effect.

Serve a variety on individual plates, or put a large plate of mixed hors d'oeuvre on the table and allow everybody to help themselves, just as you wish, or as space permits. Personally, I find it easier to arrange individual plates, and put them on the table before the guests are seated, which allows you to sit down at the same time with your guests.

## SAVOURY EGGS

Serve these either as an hors d'oeuvre or as a party savoury. They can be prepared in the morning, wrapped in plastic and stored in the refrigerator until ready to serve – but do not prepare them more than twelve hours ahead.

Eggs can be stuffed with a variety of fillings, including finely chopped anchovies; mashed sardines; grated cheese with a little mustard added; curry powder and chutney added to the yolks; chopped chives and cottage cheese; minced ham with a little mustard; finely chopped celery and chopped olives.

Boil the eggs gently for 10 minutes, then cover with cold water until cool. Shell and cut each egg in halves. Scoop the yolks into a basin and mash until smooth with whatever filling you are using. Or you may divide the yolks into two basins and make two different fillings. Use a little top milk or mayonnaise to moisten filling if necessary, and season well. Fill egg whites with the prepared mixture, and garnish with either capers, tiny sprigs of parsley, finely chopped salted peanuts, or a sprinkle of paprika.

If serving as hors d'oeuvre, turn the eggs filled-side downwards on lettuce leaves, and mask with just a little mayonnaise, then add a sprinkle of paprika.

## DRESSED RAW MUSHROOMS

These are best prepared in the morning before leaving home. They can be served as an hors d'oeuvre on lettuce leaves, and garnished with roughly chopped anchovy fillets; or well-drained and served with the savouries for a sherry or cocktail party (stick cocktail sticks into them for easy handling).

Wash and drain $\frac{1}{2}$ lb mushroom caps, but do not peel. Slice them fairly thin and put into a bowl with a clove of garlic, and a dressing made with 2 parts of salad or olive oil to 1 part lemon juice. Sprinkle with pepper, but do not add salt until just before serving. Toss the mushrooms well in the dressing, and stand until ready to serve at night. Do not put into refrigerator, but stand in a cool place.

These are also good as a garnish for a chicken salad.

## GARLIC OLIVES

Some days before serving, put a peeled clove of garlic into a bottle of either green or black olives (not stuffed), seal again and shake well several times during the time before they are needed.

This gives a delicious flavour to the olives if you are one of those people who like garlic.

## CRAB IN CUCUMBER CUPS

These make a tasty hors d'oeuvre of the salad type, and are a good beginning for a summer dinner. The cups can be prepared in the morning and left to drain, then filled just before serving. Stand each cucumber cup on a slice of tomato, well seasoned with salt and pepper and a dash of sugar. Cold, cooked green beans, dressed with an oil and vinegar dressing, go well as an accompaniment to this dish.

Choose long, straight cucumbers with smooth skins. Cut in 1½-inch lengths and scoop out the seeds with a pointed teaspoon to form cups, leaving a solid base of cucumber. Season with salt and pepper and turn upside-down on a plate to drain until ready to fill. Drain a can of crabmeat and flake well, carefully removing the hard membranes and any bits of shell. Mix with just enough mayonnaise to bind together, add 1 tablespoon finely chopped celery or chives, and season well. Fill cucumber cups with this mixture, after first removing skin from cucumbers. Add a dash of paprika to each filled cup. Serve on tomato slices or small lettuce leaves.

## BAKED GRAPEFRUIT

This can hardly be called an hors d'oeuvre, but it makes a delicious beginning to a good dinner. The grapefruit can be prepared in the morning before leaving home, then the filling replaced in the grapefruit shells just before dinner. They are best baked in individual ovenproof ramekins if available, otherwise stand grapefruit in a shallow ovenproof dish to bake, then transfer to a sweet dish to serve. They need to be baked for about 10 minutes in a fairly hot oven (400° F or No 6).

| | |
|---|---|
| 3 *large grapefruit* | *sherry* |
| 1 *cup crushed pineapple* | 6 *cherries or pieces of crystal-* |
| *brown sugar* | *lized ginger* |

Cut grapefruit in halves and cut out the pulp. Carefully remove seeds and coarse membranes and chop pulp. Put into a bowl with the crushed pineapple and sherry and leave until ready to bake. Place grapefruit shells in the ramekins and fill with grapefruit and pineapple mixture. Sprinkle top with brown sugar and dot with butter. Bake for 10 minutes, until hot and bubbling, but be careful they do not burn on top. Serve at once, garnished with cherries or ginger.

## CHICKEN AND MUSHROOM CAPS

Serve three or four of these on rounds of crisp fried bread as a hot hors d'oeuvre. The mushrooms can be prepared in the morning, the chicken chopped and the almonds blanched and chopped the night before – but do not fill mushrooms until just before putting into the oven. They need about

15 to 20 minutes heating in a moderately hot oven (375° F or No 5).

Wash and drain the mushrooms after removing the stems, but do not peel. The mushrooms should be fairly small, with nice tight cups. Make the filling with finely chopped chicken and chopped almonds, blended together with a little cream. Season to taste and fill the mushroom caps, then add a small pat of butter to each one. Place on a lightly greased oven tray and bake until mushrooms are cooked.

If chicken is being served as the main course, a filling for the mushrooms can be made with chopped ham, or finely shredded crabmeat instead of chicken. A little sherry added to the crab instead of cream is an improvement.

## FRIED SALMON PUFFS

These little puffs can be prepared in the morning, just ready to be fried in deep hot fat before serving for a buffet party. Or they can be served as the first course for dinner, garnished with lemon wedges.

| | |
|---|---|
| 8 *oz can of salmon* | 2 *oz plain flour* |
| *salt and pepper* | 2 *beaten eggs* |
| 1 *teaspoon lemon juice* | *fat for frying* |
| 1 *dessertspoon chopped parsley* | *paprika to garnish* |

Flake the salmon, removing any bones and dark skin. Add lemon juice, seasoning and parsley. Beat flour into eggs, then add salmon mixture to make a soft mixture which will drop easily off a spoon. Drop spoonfuls of the mixture into hot fat and fry until golden brown. Drain on kitchen paper and serve at once, sprinkled with paprika. Stick cocktail picks into each one if serving for a buffet party.

If preferred, flaked crab or tuna can be used instead of salmon.

# TASTY DIPS

For a buffet party a selection of dips on the table is a welcome idea. It is amazing how quickly people become friendly when they are both dipping into the same bowl.

These dips can be made up in the morning, then chilled until ready to serve. Place each mixture in an attractive bowl standing on a large platter, and surround with either potato crisps, fingers of freshly made toast, or small cream cracker or cheese flavoured biscuits, for people to help themselves.

An electric blender is a great help when making these dips.

*Anchovy Dip:* 2 oz can of anchovy fillets, drained and finely chopped, 2 teaspoons lemon juice, 4 oz cream cheese, 2 teaspoons milk. Have cream cheese at room temperature before mixing, then blend all ingredients together until smooth. Season well with pepper. If mixture is too thick, add a little more milk.

*Avocado Spread:* 1 large, ripe avocado, 3 tablespoons finely chopped celery, 3 finely chopped shallots or spring onions, 2 thin slices green pepper, chopped fine, 3 tablespoons mayonnaise, salt and black pepper, dash of lemon juice. Cut avocado in halves, remove stone, peel and mash the pulp with the lemon juice until smooth. Add remainder of ingredients, mix well and pile into bowl for serving.

*Liver and Onion Dip:* $\frac{1}{2}$ lb liver sausage, 1 tablespoon grated onion, 2 teaspoons Worcester sauce, 1 tablespoon fried, finely chopped bacon pieces, little top milk if necessary, salt and pepper. Blend all ingredients except bacon pieces together until smooth and creamy, then add bacon pieces and pile into serving bowl.

*Blue Cheese Dip:* Blend 6 oz cottage cheese and 2 oz Gorgonzola or Danish Blue cheese together, adding a little top milk if necessary to get a good spreading consistency. Add 2 tablespoons finely chopped celery and 1 tablespoon finely chopped chives, and a dash of cayenne and mix well. Pile into a serving bowl, and just before taking to the table, sprinkle top with finely chopped walnuts.

## SIMPLE PARTY SAVOURIES

Here are some suggestions for making simple savouries to serve when friends call in for drinks before dinner or on Sunday morning, and only small snacks are needed.

*Cheese and Nut Toast:* Toast required number of bread slices, and butter while hot. Sprinkle with grated cheese, season with a little paprika and add a sprinkle of chopped, blanched almonds. Put under fairly hot grill just until cheese is melted. Cut in fingers and serve at once.

*Anchovy Fingers:* Cut freshly made toast into fingers. Open a large tin of anchovies, drain well and put anchovies through a sieve, or mash well until smooth. Mix with an equal amount of unsalted butter, adding a few grains of cayenne, and use as a spread for the toast fingers. Sprinkle with a little chopped hard-boiled egg.

*Cheese and Gherkin Biscuits:* Grate some tasty cheese and mix to a rough paste with a little mayonnaise or salad dressing. Add a few chopped gherkins or chopped, stoned black olives, and spread on plain biscuits or fingers of toast.

*Piquant Crab Fingers:* Open a can of crab, drain well and shred the crab, removing any hard membranes. Season well with pepper and a few drops of lemon juice, then bind into a paste with some mayonnaise, but do not make it too moist. Spread on buttered toast fingers or on plain biscuits.

## DEVILLED ALMONDS

Prepare these any time you have some spare minutes, then store in an airtight jar until needed. If they should lose their crispness, put into the oven for a few minutes when it is hot.

1 *lb shelled almonds*          *salt*
1 *gill olive oil*               *cayenne*

Place almonds in a saucepan, cover with water and bring to
the boil. Drain immediately, and as soon as almonds are cool
enough to handle, peel off the skins. Spread out on a clean
tea-towel to dry. Heat oil in a shallow frying pan and fry
almonds until golden brown, stirring occasionally with a
fork. Lift out with a slotted spoon and drain on kitchen paper.
Put salt and cayenne into a paper bag and toss the almonds
while still hot to coat evenly.

If these are not to be served on the same day, cool completely before storing in jar.

# CHEESE PARTY-BISCUITS

Make up a quantity of these biscuits, in various shapes, and
with an assortment of garnishings, then store in an airtight
tin or jar and you always have something savoury to serve in
a hurry. Or the biscuits can be prepared in the morning,
then stored in refrigerator until just before they are needed.
They are then baked and served hot with before-dinner
drinks.

BASIC BISCUIT RECIPE
6 *oz plain flour*                    4 *oz butter or margarine*
2 *oz self-raising flour*             3 *oz grated tasty cheese*
¼ *teaspoon salt*                     1 *egg yolk*
*pinch cayenne*                       *little milk to mix*

Sift dry ingredients into a bowl, rub in fat until mixture resembles fine breadcrumbs, add cheese. Add beaten egg yolk
and just enough milk to make a firm dough. Turn out on a
lightly floured board, knead lightly. Roll out about ¼-inch
thick and cut into shapes or roll in balls as desired. Lift

carefully on to greased oven trays, bake in moderately hot oven (375° F or No 5) for 12 to 15 minutes. Loosen with a spatula and allow to cool on trays. When quite cold, store in tin.

VARIATIONS

*Cheese Meringue Biscuits:* Cut biscuit dough into small rounds and place on oven tray. Beat egg white (left over from yolk used in basic recipe) with a pinch of salt until stiff, and spread roughly on each biscuit round. Sprinkle top with a little finely grated Parmesan cheese. Bake for 12 to 15 minutes in a 375° oven. Serve hot or cold – but these will not keep well more than 12 hours.

*Ham Slices:* Roll out a little thinner than usual, but be careful not to break the dough. Shape into a rectangle. On one half brush dough over with a little made mustard, then sprinkle with finely chopped ham. Carefully spread other half of dough over the top of the ham, and with a rolling pin, roll over lightly to press two halves together evenly. Cut into slices about 1-inch wide and bake as directed.

*Crunchy Cheese Balls:* Spoon out small pieces of the biscuit dough and roll between floured hands to form balls about the size of a marble. Roll in finely grated tasty cheese, place on greased trays and bake in a slower oven (350° F or No 4) for 15 to 20 minutes, or until golden brown.

As a change, roll the balls of biscuit dough in finely chopped nuts instead of cheese.

*Caraway Rounds:* Cut rolled-out dough into small rounds, brush each one over with beaten egg-white, and sprinkle with caraway seeds. Bake as directed.

*Cheese Pinwheels:* Cut the rolled-out dough into 4-inch squares. Sprinkle thickly with grated cheese and add a dash of mustard. Roll up each square like a Swiss roll, pressing lightly but firmly together. Cut each roll into $\frac{1}{4}$-inch thick slices, and place on greased baking tray. Bake as directed. These are best served hot.

25

## CHEESE AND CELERY MARBLES

These are best made in the morning and chilled in the refrigerator until time to serve.

8 *oz cream cheese*　　　　　　　1 *tablespoon mayonnaise*
1 *tablespoon finely chopped celery*　*finely chopped parsley or chives*
*dash of cayenne*

Beat cheese well to soften and beat in mayonnaise. Add celery and cayenne and beat again until well blended. Form mixture into small balls, about the size of a marble, and roll in finely chopped parsley or chives. Put into 'fridge until ready to serve on cocktail sticks.

## CHEESE DELIGHTS

Make these tasty biscuits just about bite-size, and serve with pre-dinner drinks.

4 *oz shredded tasty cheese*　　　½ *teaspoon salt*
2 *oz butter*　　　　　　　　　　*pinch cayenne*
3 *oz plain flour*　　　　　　　　½ *teaspoon Worcestershire sauce*

Sift flour, salt and cayenne together. Cream butter and cheese together, add sauce, and blend well, then add dry ingredients. Chill this mixture until firm enough to roll into small balls about the size of marbles. Place on a greased baking sheet and flatten with the prongs of a fork. Chill for a further 20 minutes, then bake in a hot oven (450° F or No 8) for 10 minutes, or until lightly browned.

For a change, sprinkle top of each biscuit with poppy seeds; or place a salted peanut in centre of each one before baking.

# ASPARAGUS ROLLS

Drain a can of asparagus tips for some hours before using. (Retain the juice for soup or a sauce.) Cut thin slices of fresh brown bread and remove crusts, then spread with smoothly blended cottage cheese. Cut each slice in half, making two squares, and place an asparagus tip crosswise on the bread square. Roll up as firmly as possible from one corner to the other, and pack the rolls into a plastic bag, join downwards, as you make them.

Store in refrigerator until ready to serve. These can be made in the morning, ready to be served at night.

# STUFFED PICKLED CUCUMBERS

Choose large pickled cucumbers as well-formed and straight as possible. Cut a thin slice from each end, and with an apple corer remove the middle of each cucumber. (Use the middles, chopped, to add to flaked salmon as a sandwich filling). Blend cottage or cream cheese with finely chopped chives, and a dash of cayenne. Drain the cucumbers well, then stuff with the cheese mixture. Wrap in greaseproof paper or foil and chill until ready to serve, then cut in $\frac{1}{2}$-inch slices. Insert a cocktail stick in each slice to serve.

# Soups

During cold weather soups make a very important beginning to a meal, and they are many and varied to suit any menu. Iced soups are also good with summer meals.

There are two main types of soups, those made with meat and bone stock, and those made with vegetables and thickened with cream, milk and flour. There is also another type which has its place in today's meals, the soup which comes out of a can or a packet, or is made with soup cubes. This type is especially useful for the businesswoman-housewife.

A first course of soup improves the digestion and also stimulates the appetite, and increases the variety of a meal. It can also provide the main dish for a light meal, served for supper in front of the fire, or for lunch when the main meal is at night, and on such occasions a hearty soup such as Tomato-Corn Chowder (page 36) or Mulligatawny (page 30) is recommended.

Gravy left in a casserole, vegetables left over from dinner, or the carcase of a chicken can all be used as the base for a tasty soup, and the addition of a beef cube to the water drained from cooked vegetables makes a quick consommé.

I have included here several suggestions for simple and quickly prepared soups made with soup cubes or with canned soup, any of which would be very useful when unexpected guests arrive and the cupboard is rather bare.

## MUSHROOM AND POTATO SOUP

A thick, creamy soup made with mushrooms can be a

delicious beginning for a meal, or it makes a good supper dish served with toasted cheese fingers, eaten in front of a big fire on a cold night.

½ *lb potatoes, peeled and sliced*  ½ *lb mushrooms, chopped*
1 *stalk of celery, chopped*  ½ *oz butter*
2 *onions, sliced*  ½ *pint milk*
1 *pint boiling water*  *salt and pepper to taste*

Cook the potatoes, onions and celery together with the salted water until tender. Put the whole mixture through a sieve, cool and store in refrigerator overnight.

Do not peel the mushrooms, but chop stalks and tops separately. Melt butter in a saucepan and cook the stalks for a few minutes, then add remainder of mushrooms and cook for a further 3 minutes, stirring occasionally to cook evenly in the butter. Add the potato mixture, blend well, then add milk. Season to taste and simmer for 8 minutes, stirring occasionally. Serve at once.

## CREAM OF CHESTNUT SOUP

When chestnuts are available, this creamy soup with its rather unusual flavour is very welcome on a cold winter's night.

1 *lb chestnuts*  ¼ *pint milk*
1 *oz butter or margarine*  1 *tablespoon plain flour*
1 *small onion, sliced*  ½ *teaspoon sugar*
1½ *pints chicken stock (made with*  *salt and pepper to taste*
    *cubes if necessary)*  3 *tablespoons cream or top milk*
 *chopped parsley or chives*

Make a slit in each chestnut at both ends with a sharp knife. Cover with water, bring to boil and boil for about 10 minutes, then drain and peel while still hot. Slice or chop the peeled chestnuts. Melt butter or margarine in saucepan and fry the sliced onion and chestnuts for a few minutes, then add stock, cover and simmer until chestnuts are quite tender, about an hour. Put mixture through a sieve or electric blender, cool and store in a covered jar in refrigerator.

Next day, bring chestnut soup to boiling point. Blend flour with milk and add to soup, stirring until it boils. Cook for 3 minutes, taste for seasoning, then stir in cream or top milk and serve at once, sprinkled with chopped parsley or chives.

## MULLIGATAWNY SOUP

A thick tasty soup for those who like the flavour of curry.

| | |
|---|---|
| 2 *onions* | 2 *oz flour* |
| 1 *large carrot* | 1 *quart stock (made with cubes* |
| 1 *cooking apple* | *if necessary)* |
| 1 *small turnip* | *bouquet garni* |
| 2 *rashers bacon* | *salt and pepper* |
| 1 *oz butter or margarine* | 1 *teaspoon lemon juice* |
| 1 *tablespoon curry powder* | *chopped parsley* |

Peel and chop the vegetables and the apple. Cut rind from bacon, and cut bacon into small pieces, frying lightly in a large saucepan until lightly browned. Add butter or margarine to fat in pan and fry vegetables and apple for a few minutes, then stir in curry powder and flour and cook for a minute. Now gradually stir in the stock and bring to the boil, add bouquet garni and simmer gently for 1 hour, skimming occasionally if necessary. Remove bouquet garni and put soup through a sieve or electric blender. Put aside in refrigerator until next day.

When ready to cook, heat soup just to boiling point, taste

for seasoning, and add lemon juice. Sprinkle each serve with a little parsley. If liked, some cooked rice can be added to the soup when it is re-heated.

## QUICK VEGETABLE SOUP

This useful soup can be made right from scratch in under half an hour, or in less time if you have prepared the vegetables in the morning before leaving home. Either meat stock or bouillon cubes can be used.

| | |
|---|---|
| 1 *large onion* | 2 *pints stock* |
| 2 *carrots* | *salt and pepper to taste* |
| 1 *small parsnip* | *chopped parsley* |
| 1 *small turnip* | *rice or noodles* (optional) |
| 1 *stalk of celery* | |

Wash and peel the root vegetables, scrub the celery, and either coarsely grate or finely chop them all. Add to heated stock and simmer, covered, for 10 to 15 minutes until vegetables are tender. Taste for seasoning and add chopped parsley. Serve at once.

If desired, rice or noodles may be cooked with the vegetables to give more body to the soup.

If a cream soup is wanted, add 1 cup milk to vegetables in saucepan and thicken mixture with 1 heaped tablespoon flour blended with a little milk and stirred into the soup until it thickens.

## CREAM OF SHRIMP SOUP

This is a delicious soup to make the day after you have been poaching fish (as in Fish Mallorquina, page 41), and have a quantity of fish stock left. The fish stock should be strained and stored in a covered jar in the refrigerator, but do not keep for more than 24 hours before using. Keep the bones and trimmings from the fish and add to the stock with a large chopped tomato, or 2 teaspoons of tomato paste, and simmer together, covered, for 20 minutes. Strain, cool and refrigerate until ready to make and serve.

Measure the stock, bringing quantity up to 2 pints with milk. Blend 2 teaspoons cornflour with a little milk until smooth, bring stock to boil and stir in blended cornflour, stirring until thickened. Have ready desired quantity of shelled, roughly chopped shrimps and add to soup. Cook for five minutes, stirring occasionally, then serve at once.

# CHEESE CHOWDER

A nourishing, creamy soup which is especially good for the children when they come home cold on a winter's day. If the vegetables are prepared the night before and put into plastic bags in the refrigerator, this soup does not take more than 15 minutes to cook when you come home.

| | |
|---|---|
| ½ *cup coarsely grated carrot* | 2½ *cups milk* |
| ½ *cup chopped celery* | 1 *cup coarsely grated cheese* |
| 2 *tablespoons chopped onion* | *salt and pepper* |
| 1½ *cups boiling water* | *chopped celery leaves* |
| 1½ *oz butter or margarine* | *sprinkle of paprika* |
| 2 *tablespoons plain flour* | |

Cook carrot and celery in boiling salted water for 10 minutes. While vegetables are cooking fry onion in the butter or margarine until tender, but do not brown. Stir in flour and cook together for a few minutes. Gradually stir in the milk, and continue stirring until mixture boils. Add vegetables and water in which they were cooked.

If making the night before serving, allow mixture to cool and store in refrigerator until needed. Re-heat and stir in cheese until it has melted and blended with mixture. Serve at once, sprinkle with chopped celery leaves.

If serving at once, bring mixture back to boiling point, then stir in cheese and chopped celery leaves and stir until cheese has melted.

## CREAMED ONION SOUP

This can be made up the night before and re-heated when ready to serve, or it takes so little time to prepare that you could make it up when you come home if necessary.

4 *large onions*
4 *oz butter or margarine*
*salt and pepper*

1½ *pints milk (or milk and*
   *water mixed)*
1 *tablespoon cream*
*grated cheese*

Peel onions and slice very thinly. Cook in the hot butter until pale golden and transparent, but do not allow to brown. Pour in milk, or milk and water and simmer for 15 minutes, seasoning to taste.

If making the night before, pour soup into a bowl, cool and store in refrigerator until ready to serve. Re-heat, stirring occasionally, then add cream and pour into four soup bowls. Sprinkle liberally with grated cheese.

## CHICKEN BROTH

This is a good way to follow up a boiled fowl next day, using the carcase and the stock in which the bird was cooked. It improves by being made the night before, as the fat can be skimmed off the cold stock before re-heating to serve.

B                          33

carcase of chicken, and trimmings
2½ pints stock, or stock and water
  mixed
1 medium onion, chopped
1 medium carrot, chopped
1 stalk of celery (if available)
½ cup chopped chicken meat
2 tablespoons rice
chopped parsley
salt and pepper to taste

Break up the carcase and put with trimmings, skin, etc., into a saucepan with stock and water, onion, carrot and celery, and simmer covered, for 45 minutes. Strain, and when cold store stock in refrigerator in a covered container.

Next day, skim off any fat, and bring stock to boil. Slowly add the well-washed rice and simmer until rice is tender, about 15 minutes. Add chicken pieces and parsley, re-heat for 2 minutes, and serve.

The carcase of a duck can be used in the same way to make broth. If preferred, noodles can be used instead of rice, or both can be omitted and the soup served clear with only the chicken pieces and parsley.

# ICED CONSOMME JULIENNE

During the warm weather a bowl of iced soup, garnished with colourful vegetables, not only tempts the appetite but also adds eye-appeal to the meal.

There are many winter soups which can be given a 'new dress' for the summer by adding a little gelatine and serving well chilled, but choose only thin soups for this method – cream soups are rarely satisfactory. Serve the soup in consommé cups or bowls rather than in large soup plates, and garnish with chopped chives, chopped cucumber or chopped tomato for colour and flavour.

This is a simple soup which makes a good beginning to a summer meal.

1¼ *pints clear meat stock (made with bouillon cubes if necessary)*
1 *small onion*
1 *stalk of celery*
1 *small carrot*
1 *tablespoon gelatine*
*salt and pepper*

Shred the carrot and celery into thin strands. Chop onion very small. Cook vegetables in ¼ pint boiling water until tender. If using bouillon cubes, dissolve in 1 pint of hot water, stir in the gelatine, making sure it is completely dissolved, then add cooled vegetables and water in which they were cooked. Otherwise, dissolve gelatine in pint of stock and continue as above. Taste for seasoning. When cold, store in refrigerator to set overnight.

When ready to serve divide mixture between four bowls or cups, breaking up roughly with a fork.

# VICHYSSOISE

This classic French soup is one of the few thick soups which can be served chilled. It is delicious either hot or cold.

6 *large leeks*
4 *tablespoons butter or margarine*
4 *medium-size potatoes*
1½ *pints chicken stock (made with cubes if necessary)*
*salt and pepper*
*pinch of ground nutmeg*
½ *pint cream*
*chopped chives*

Use only the white parts of the leeks, and cut into 1-inch lengths, washing very well to remove all sand. Sauté in butter or margarine until soft, but do not allow to brown.

Peel and slice potatoes and add to leeks with chicken stock and seasonings, and simmer until vegetables are soft. Force through a fine sieve or put through an electric blender.

If serving hot, store sieved mixture in refrigerator overnight, then re-heat and stir in cream. Serve at once sprinkled with chives.

If serving cold, chill overnight, then just before serving stir in cream and divide between four or five soup bowls and sprinkle with chives.

## CHILLED BORSCHT

A delightfully coloured and flavoured soup to serve as the first course for a summer dinner party. If you have glass bowls serve the borscht in these, and float a tablespoon of sour cream or yoghurt on top of each bowl of soup.

| | |
|---|---|
| 5 *or* 6 *medium-size beetroot* | 2 *pints cold water* |
| 1 *medium onion, chopped* | 1½ *teaspoons salt* |
| 1 *medium cooking apple, chopped* | 1 *teaspoon sugar* |
| 1½ *cups shredded cabbage* | *sour cream or yoghurt* |

Scrub beetroot well after cutting off leafy tops without cutting into the beetroot. Coarsely grate them into a saucepan (to retain all the juices), and add onion, apple and cabbage, water and salt. Bring to boil and simmer for 1 hour. Strain into a bowl, pressing mixture with a spoon to extract all the juice. Add sugar, using more if necessary. The borscht should have a slightly sweet-sour taste. Cool and chill in refrigerator until ready to serve next day. Taste before serving and add a little lemon juice if necessary.

## TOMATO-CORN CHOWDER

This is quickly and easily prepared and makes a tasty and filling soup for winter suppers.

10½ oz can of condensed tomato soup
1 pint milk
1 small can cream-style sweet corn

½ teaspoon curry powder
1 tablespoon chopped parsley
grated cheese

Combine all ingredients except cheese and heat without allowing to boil. Serve sprinkled with grated cheese. To serve 6.

## QUICK CRAB CHOWDER

For a quick and really delicious chowder for a special guest this is the easiest soup I know.

Combine 1 can condensed tomato soup, 1 can condensed cream of asparagus soup, 1 small can of crab meat (carefully remove any fibres, then flake the fish), and 1 soup can of milk. Heat without allowing to boil, taste for seasoning and serve in heated soup bowls, with a slice of lemon floating on top of each bowl. To serve 6.

## CONSOMME CELESTINE

Another quickly made soup which looks and tastes good. This is an excellent soup to make the day following a serving of pancakes, as 2 or 3 extra can be made and kept in a covered container in the refrigerator, ready for this soup.

Make 1 quart of chicken broth, using cubes if necessary. Roll up the pancakes (for recipe see page 162), and with a very sharp knife cut rolls crosswise into fine shreds. Shake them out to separate, then add to hot soup and serve at once. Soup may be garnished with chopped parsley, chopped chives or grated Parmesan cheese as desired.

# EGG DROP SOUP

A very popular Chinese soup which is most useful in an emergency when unexpected guests arrive for a meal.

Make 1 quart of chicken broth, using cubes if necessary, and heat it in a large saucepan. Beat 3 or 4 eggs until light and frothy, and pour in a thin stream into the boiling soup, whisking constantly all the time. Add 2 teaspoons soya sauce if available, season to taste and simmer for no longer than 1 minute.

Serve in deep, heated bowls, garnished with chopped chives or finely chopped scallions or spring onions.

# Fish

The fish recipes given in this chapter are all ones which need some preparation beforehand, either the night before or in the morning before leaving home.

I have not given the usual ways of cooking fish, such as grilling, frying and poaching, which must be done immediately before serving, as they are too well known to need repeating. But in the chapter on Sauces and Dressings there are a number of tasty sauces which can be made ahead of time and heated just before serving and which are excellent with grilled or fried fish.

Great care must be taken when storing fish overnight. Do not attempt to keep it unless you have a refrigerator, because even cooked fish can quickly 'go off' if the weather is at all warm. To prevent the fish smell from going through your refrigerator, wrap the fish carefully in cooking foil, seal well and store in the tray underneath the freezing unit.

## COD STEAKS PORTUGAISE

The frozen cod steaks obtainable four in a packet (14 oz) are excellent for this dish, but I find one cod steak is not quite enough for most men, so allow for this and use one small and one large packet – 6 steaks – for four good serves. The tomato mixture can be prepared and cooked the night before, then refrigerated until next day when you are ready to cook the meal. The fish are grilled and take only about 8 minutes on each side when unthawed, or less if thawed.

Serve with a green vegetable and small new potatoes cooked and tossed in butter and chopped parsley.

| | |
|---|---|
| 1 *lb tomatoes, peeled and sliced* | *salt and pepper* |
| 1 *medium onion, sliced* | ½ *teaspoon sugar* |
| 1 *clove of garlic (if liked)* | 1 *tablespoon cooking oil* |
| 1 *small green pepper, sliced* | 1 *dessertspoon butter* |
| *pinch mixed herbs* | *cod steaks* |

Heat the oil in a pan and cook the onion until transparent. Add tomatoes and green pepper, herbs, salt, pepper and sugar and cook all together for about 10 minutes. Cool and store until next day.

To save trouble I line the griller pan with aluminium foil, first removing the rack. Heat the tomato mixture in a small saucepan until nearly boiling, then pour into the foil-lined pan. Place the cod steaks on top, season lightly with salt and pepper and place a small pat of butter on each. Grill until pale golden and cooked half-way through, then turn to brown other side. Serve with the tomato mixture round them.

If more convenient, the cod can be baked in the oven in the same way, but it takes a little longer.


## PICKLED COD STEAKS

Cod steaks or fillets, either fresh or frozen, can be used for this recipe, which makes a tasty summer dish, served with salad and a piquant dressing.

The fish is cooked the night before, and allowed to cool in the pickling mixture overnight. In the morning it should be drained, wrapped in foil and stored in refrigerator until ready to be served for dinner.

1½ lb fish fillets
½ cup white vinegar
½ cup boiling water
3 whole cloves
3 or 4 whole peppercorns
1 bay leaf
few grains cayenne

small clove of garlic
3 or 4 thin slices onion
2 or 3 sprigs of parsley
sprigs of fresh thyme and mar-
    joram (or dried herbs)
½ teaspoon salt

Place the fish in an ovenproof casserole. Bring all other ingredients to the boil, pour over the fish and cover. Bake in a moderate oven (350° F or No 4) until fish is white and flakes easily. Uncover, and allow to cool in liquid in casserole, basting occasionally. Drain and keep in refrigerator until ready to serve.

Serve on lettuce leaves with sliced, peeled tomatoes and cucumber.

## FISH MALLORQUINA

This is a cold dish to be served on a special occasion. It looks magnificent as the centrepiece of a buffet dinner table if care is taken in garnishing it. One large whole fish or two smaller fish are needed to serve 8 to 10 people, and a large 5 lb salmon trout is excellent cooked like this.

All the cooking is done the night before, and the fish is wrapped in foil and stored in refrigerator, but it should be removed at least 15 minutes before serving time. Being served too cold spoils the flavour. It should be garnished at the last minute before taking to the table.

about 5 *lb of fish*
1 *small carrot, peeled and sliced*
1 *sliced onion*
1 *stalk of celery with leaves*
1 *large bay leaf*
6 *whole peppercorns*
1 *clove of garlic (if liked)*
3 *hard-boiled egg yolks*
1 *tablespoon capers*
1 *tablespoon chopped chives or*
　1 *dessertspoon grated onion*
2 *sprigs of parsley*

2 *tablespoons olive oil*
2 *tablespoons wine vinegar*
1 *dessertspoon sugar*
1 *tablespoon chopped parsley*
*salt to taste*
*few grains cayenne*
1½ *cups fish stock*
*cooked carrot slices*
*cooked peas*
*asparagus spears*
*canned pimento slices*

Have the fishmonger clean the fish for you, but it must be left whole. Wrap the fish in a square of muslin to enable it to be lifted from the saucepan without breaking, and be sure to use a saucepan or boiler large enough to cook the fish whole.

Put the sliced carrot, onion, sliced celery, bay leaf, peppercorns, sprigs of parsley, 1 teaspoon salt, garlic (if using) and 2 quarts of cold water into the saucepan and bring to the boil, then simmer for 30 minutes. Allow the pan to go off the boil and carefully lower the wrapped fish into the stock. Simmer gently for 15 to 20 minutes, until fish is cooked through, but cooking time depends on thickness of fish, so test one small portion to make sure it is cooked. If cooked for too long, the fish will break up and lose its shape. Lift the fish carefully from the pan by the muslin wrapping and place it on the platter on which you will bring it to the table. Remove the skin very carefully, keeping the fish a good shape.

Strain the stock and put 1½ cupfuls aside. If you have an electric blender you will have no trouble making the sauces; if not, chop the egg yolks, parsley, capers, chives or onion as small as possible, add the oil, vinegar and fish stock and blend into a sauce. Taste for seasoning. While the fish is still warm pour half the sauce over it, and baste occasionally as it cools. Put remainder of sauce in a covered jar in refrigerator until next day.

Chill overnight, and when ready to serve garnish the fish with alternate carrot and pimento slices down each side, and arrange cold cooked peas in lettuce cups around the dish, with asparagus spears as extra garnishing. Put remainder of sauce in a sauce-boat and hand round separately. Mayonnaise can also be served if liked.

Cut down the centre of the fish and remove backbone when fish is to be served.


## FISH TURBANS IN TOMATO CASES

Fresh or frozen fillets can be used for this recipe, plaice being suitable. The ingredients are prepared in the morning, ready to be cooked for 20 minutes at night for dinner. Serve with oven-browned potatoes (page 125) and a green vegetable. Allow 1 large tomato and 2 fish fillets for each serve.

| | |
|---|---|
| *tomatoes* | *mixed herbs* |
| *fish fillets* | *salt and pepper* |
| 1 *cup dry white wine or cider* | *grated Parmesan cheese* |
| *butter* | *lemon wedges* |

In the morning place fish fillets in a shallow dish and pour wine or cider over them. Stand in a cool place (not in refrigerator) until ready to cook. Cut each tomato in halves, carefully scoop out the pulp without piercing the outer skin. Season with salt and pepper and turn upside-down to drain.

When ready to cook, drain fillets and roll each one from head to tail to make a turban. Sprinkle tomato cases with a very little of the mixed herbs, and place a fish turban in each half tomato. Sprinkle with Parmesan cheese and add a dab of butter. Place each one in a greased patty tin in order to keep them upright. Bake in a moderately hot oven (375° F or No 5) for 20 minutes. Garnish with lemon wedges to serve.

## FISH IN FOIL

The sauce in this recipe can be made the night before and stored in refrigerator until fish is ready to cook. Cooking time is about 20 minutes, for the fish in foil parcels.

8 *to* 10 *small fish fillets*
2 *tablespoons finely chopped onion*
½ *lb mushrooms, chopped*
6 *tablespoons butter or cooking oil*
1 *large tomato, peeled and seeded*

2 *tablespoons flour*
*salt and pepper to taste*
6 *tablespoons thick cream*
*small pinch mixed herbs*
2 *tablespoons parsley, chopped*

Melt 2 tablespoons butter in a thick saucepan and sauté the onion, mushrooms, chopped tomato, and parsley until onion is transparent. Blend in flour then add cream gradually, stirring all the time. Season to taste, add herbs and bring to boil, then simmer until sauce is thick, stirring occasionally. When required consistency, allow to cool. Store it, covered, in refrigerator until next day.

When ready to cook dinner, season fillets with salt and pepper and sauté in remaining butter, browning lightly on both sides. Have 4 pieces of cooking foil cut into rectangles or ovals about 8 by 10 inches, and brush over the inside of each with cooking oil. Crease each oval through the middle. Heat up the sauce by standing bowl over simmering water until hot but not boiling.

Put a spoonful of the sauce on one half of each foil oval and arrange 2 or 3 fish fillets on top, then cover with more sauce. Fold foil over and seal the edges well by crimping or folding together. Prepare remainder of foil ovals in the same way. Place on a baking sheet and bake in a moderately hot oven (375° F or No 5) for 15 minutes.

To serve, slit each parcel open and roll edges back without allowing the sauce to spill out.

## MACARONI ALLA MARINIERA

A very useful dish to serve for an informal dinner party, this is also a change from the more usual spaghetti dishes which many people serve on such occasions. The sauce is prepared the night before, and can be re-heated while the macaroni is cooking ready to serve at once.

The sauce can be used with macaroni, spaghetti or even over rice, but the pasta I prefer for this is the Italian one called 'gozzetoni', which is made in the shape of shells, and which holds the well-flavoured sauce and looks decorative.

Any coarse fish can be used, or use a mixture of cod and chopped scallops and throw in a few shelled prawns as well, just as you please. The fish should be poached.

| | |
|---|---|
| 1 *lb cooked fish* | 1 *bay leaf* |
| 1 *cup fish stock* | ½ *teaspoon mixed, dried herbs (or* |
| 1 *clove of garlic (if liked)* | *fresh ones if available)* |
| 4 *medium onions, sliced* | ¼ *lb mushrooms, chopped* |
| 2 *tablespoons cooking oil* | *salt and pepper to taste* |
| 1 *lb tomatoes, peeled* | 1 *lb macaroni shells* |
| 2 *oz tomato paste* | *chopped parsley to garnish* |

Make the sauce by heating the oil in a thick pan and lightly browning the garlic, which should then be discarded. Brown the sliced onions, but do not burn, then add chopped tomatoes, herbs, tomato paste and seasonings. Simmer all together for 20 minutes, while the fish is poaching. Drain the fish well and cool. Strain the fish stock and add 1 cupful of the stock to the sauce, with the mushrooms. Cover and simmer for about 1 hour, stirring occasionally. A little more stock may be added if the sauce is too thick. Press the sauce through a sieve or cool and put through an electric blender. Store in refrigerator in a covered container. Wrap the fish in cooking foil and store in the coldest part of refrigerator.

When ready to prepare meal flake the fish, removing any dark skin and bones. Put macaroni on to cook in boiling, salted water, and cook for 10 to 12 minutes, until tender but not soft. The shells should keep their shape when drained. Put into a heated serving bowl. Heat the sauce, add the flaked fish and bring just to boiling point, then pour over macaroni. Stir lightly, sprinkle with finely choppd parsley, and serve at once.

## PRAWN AND EGG CURRY

The curry sauce of this recipe can be made the night before, and the eggs cooked, leaving only the re-heating of the sauce and the rice to be cooked next day. Any cooked, flaked fish can be used in place of prawns if preferred.

6 *oz peeled prawns*
4 *hard-boiled eggs*
1½ *oz butter or margarine*
4 *shallots or a small onion*
1 *tablespoon curry powder (or to taste)*
1 *tablespoon flour*
*boiled rice*

1 *pint fish or chicken stock*
1 *clove of garlic (if liked)*
1 *dessertspoon red currant jelly*
1 *tablespoon blanched chopped almonds*
*salt and pepper to taste*
3 *tablespoons cream*

Melt the butter in a thick pan and cook the chopped shallots or onion until pale golden. Blend in curry powder and cook for 3 minutes, then stir in flour and blend well. Pour on the stock slowly, stirring until blended and thickening. Add garlic and seasoning to taste, then simmer for 20 to 25 minutes, stirring occasionally. Remove garlic, cool and store in a covered jar in refrigerator until next day.

About 20 minutes before serving time, wash the rice well and cook in boiling, salted water for about 12 minutes, then drain and rinse under hot water. Re-heat the sauce over boiling water, add the prawns, almonds and red currant jelly, then carefully stir in the cream, heating the sauce up again without allowing to boil. Serve over the rice, garnished with sliced hard-boiled eggs and accompanied by cucumber raita.

## CUCUMBER RAITA

Peel a young cucumber and grate on a coarse grater. Salt lightly and leave for 15 minutes. Drain off the liquid, and mix cucumber into a cup of yoghurt or sour cream. Season with pepper or paprika. This is excellent with any plain fish dish.

## FRIED RICE WITH CRAB

This is a good dish for when an extra guest comes un-expectedly, for it can be stretched by adding more crab, and perhaps some more vegetables, such as chopped celery or chopped green or red peppers. The rice is cooked the night before and spread out on a plate to dry, ready to be fried just before serving. Either canned or freshly cooked crab can be used, and a few shelled shrimps make a nice garnish.

| | |
|---|---|
| 8 *oz rice* | 2 *cups cooked, flaked crab meat* |
| 1 *medium onion* | 2 *beaten eggs* |
| 1 *clove of garlic (if liked)* | 2 *tablespoons soya sauce* |
| 3 *tablespoons cooking oil* | $\frac{1}{2}$ *teaspoon sugar* |
| *salt and pepper* | |

Wash the rice well and cook in boiling, salted water for 10 to

12 minutes, until tender but not soggy. Drain and rinse well under cold running water, draining well again. Spread out on large plate to dry, tossing occasionally with a fork to separate grains.

When ready to cook, heat oil in thick pan and fry the sliced onion until golden. Add flaked crab meat and cook 2 minutes, turning with a fork as it cooks, then add rice and stir well into onion and crab, cooking until lightly tinted, turning often with a fork. Stir in the beaten eggs, soya sauce and sugar, and cook gently until eggs thicken. Serve at once.

## RICE AND TUNA CASSEROLE

This is an appetizing mixture of fish, rice and eggs which makes a good family meal, served with a green vegetable or baked tomatoes.

The rice and eggs are cooked the night before, and the sauce can also be prepared the night before if preferred. The dish is then put together and baked in a moderate oven for about 20 to 25 minutes.

*7 or 8 oz can of tuna (or salmon)*      *1 teaspoon Worcestershire sauce*
*2 cups medium white sauce*      *salt and pepper*
*3 cups cooked rice (1 cup un-*      *2 tablespoons chopped parsley*
*cooked)*      *½ cup grated cheese*
*3 or 4 hard-boiled eggs*

When ready to cook the casserole, heat white sauce over hot water and add flaked fish, sauce and parsley. Shell the eggs and cut in slices. Put alternate layers of rice, fish, sauce and sliced eggs in greased casserole, seasoning to taste, until all ingredients are used up. Sprinkle a thick layer of grated cheese over the top and bake in a moderate oven (350° F or No 4) until casserole is bubbling hot and top golden brown.

## FISH AND BACON KEBABS

These make a delicious savoury for a buffet party, or they can be served as a main meal on a bed of freshly cooked rice. They are cooked immediately before serving, and take about 20 minutes cooking time. Amounts depend on numbers to be served, but at least three rolls should be served to each person.

*fish fillets*  
*bacon rashers*  
*button mushrooms (if liked)*  

*salt and pepper*  
*mixed herbs*  
*steel skewers*  
*melted butter*

Cut each fillet in halves lengthwise. Sprinkle lightly with herbs, salt and pepper. Cut strips of bacon the same size as the fillets, place a strip of fish on each strip of bacon and roll up, with bacon on the outside. If mushrooms are to be used, remove the stems and wipe over the tops. Dip in melted butter. Thread alternate fish rolls and mushrooms on skewers, and grill until bacon is crisp and fish cooked through, turning frequently.

If serving on rice, cook it while the kebabs are grilling, drain and rinse well, then toss with finely chopped parsley.

## SAVOURY FISH FLAN

Any freshly poached fish can be used for this recipe, or canned salmon could be used when fresh fish is not available. The pastry flan case is made and baked the night before, and the fish can also be poached and stored well-wrapped with cooking foil in refrigerator until ready to cook. Allow 30 minutes cooking time before serving.

1 *lb fish fillets*
6 *oz short pastry*
2 *tablespoons butter or margarine*
2 *tablespoons flour*
*salt and pepper to taste*
*few grains cayenne*
2 *eggs, separated*

¾ *pint fish stock and milk mixed*
   *together*
1 *dessertspoon chopped parsley*
1 *tablespoon sherry*
1 *slice of onion*
1 *small bay leaf*
3 *whole peppercorns*
3 *sprigs of parsley*

Roll out pastry and line an 8-inch flan case. Prick all over with a fork, place a round of paper on top weighted with beans or bread crusts, and bake in a hot oven (450° F or No 7 or 8) for 15 to 20 minutes. Remove paper and beans for last 5 minutes cooking time to brown base of flan. Cool and store in an airtight tin until next day.

While the flan case is baking, poach the fish fillets. Place the onion, peppercorns, bay leaf and sprigs of parsley in a small muslin bag and tie firmly. Place the fish fillets in a saucepan with the muslin bag of seasonings, just cover with warm water, add a little salt and the sherry. Bring to the boil and simmer gently for 5 to 7 minutes, or until fish is cooked through, and flakes easily. Remove fish from saucepan, cool and wrap firmly in cooking foil, then store in refrigerator until needed next day. Strain the fish stock and when cold, store in a covered jar in refrigerator.

When ready to cook dinner, flake the fish, removing any dark skin and bones. Melt butter or margarine in small pan, blend in flour, cook for a minute then stir in fish stock and milk and continue to stir until mixture thickens and boils. Remove from heat and cool for 5 minutes, then add flaked fish, slightly beaten egg yolks, parsley, seasoning to taste, and lastly the stiffly beaten egg whites. Pour into the baked flan case and bake in a moderate oven (350° F or No 4) for 20 to 25 minutes, or until set.

Chopped red pepper, chopped cooked mushrooms or

capers can be added to the sauce for extra flavour if liked.

Serve with baked tomatoes in season, or mixed peas and diced carrots to give colour to the dish.

# Poultry

In a book such as this, when so many dishes have to be prepared and cooked or half-cooked, the day before, it is not necessary to give directions for roasting whole birds which take time to cook and are not suitable for re-heating in the oven.

But there are many other recipes which can be used for chicken pieces, which seems to be the most popular way of buying chicken these days. A whole bird can be casseroled if desired, but for the extra time needed for cooking, it hardly seems worthwhile, unless you cook it on a Sunday when you are home all day.

Included here are some recipes for using left-overs of duck and turkey which you will find useful after Christmas dinner, and these same recipes can also be used for chicken left-overs if desired.

Remember not to put a casserole straight from the refrigerator into the oven for re-heating, unless you are using an enamel or enamelled-iron one. If you haven't the time to wait for it to come back to room temperature, it is better to turn the contents of the casserole into another casserole of the same size, or even into a saucepan, to re-heat. Better to wash two casseroles than to have one shatter in the heat of the oven after the cold of the 'fridge.

## BASIC RECIPE FOR SIMPLE CASSEROLES

With the need for making a casserole in two parts, this recipe gives the initial stages of the casserole, shortening the cooking time by cooking the chicken or chicken pieces in a saucepan until just tender. The stock in which it has been cooked is then strained, and gives a good base for the sauce in which the chicken finishes cooking in a casserole. The chicken should be removed from the stock as soon as it is tender, put into a casserole and cooled, then covered and stored in refrigerator until needed. The stock is strained, cooled and also stored in 'fridge until required. In this way you should be able to serve a tasty casserole in half an hour.

If preferred, or if it is more convenient, you can make a sauce and re-heat the chicken pieces in the sauce while the vegetables are cooking. A duck can be cooked in the same way if desired, then made up into a casserole, and a larger bird can become just as tender as a young chicken cooked like this, but given more cooking time.

| | |
|---|---|
| *chicken, duck or boiling fowl* | 1 *onion, sliced* |
| *salt and peppercorns* | 1 *carrot, sliced* |
| *bay leaf* | *few sprigs of parsley* |
| 1 *stalk of celery, chopped* | *water to cover* |

If a frozen bird (or pieces) is being used, always allow to thaw before cooking. Place in saucepan with all above ingredients, bring to boil and simmer, covered, until tender, usually about $\frac{3}{4}$ to 1 hour for pieces, or longer for an older bird.

Remove from stock and store as directed above. The bird can then be finished as suggested in following recipes.


## CHICKEN CASSEROLE AU GRATIN

Prepare the chicken (as in the basic recipe, above) the night before. When tender roll each piece in seasoned flour and brown in some butter or bacon fat. Place chicken in casserole, and when quite cold, cover and store in refrigerator. Make sauce with:

| | |
|---|---|
| 3 *oz butter or margarine* | 2 *cups strained chicken stock* |
| 3 *oz flour* | 1 *cup milk* |
| *salt and pepper* | 1 *cup grated cheese* |
| | 4 *peeled and chopped tomatoes* |

Half an hour before serving time, heat the oven to 400° F. Remove chicken from refrigerator and place chopped tomatoes round it in the casserole. Make the sauce by melting butter in saucepan and blending in the flour. Cook for 2 minutes, then stir in stock and milk and bring to boil, stirring constantly. When thickened, stir in half the cheese, and season to taste. (Remember that stock has already been seasoned.) Pour over chicken in casserole and sprinkle with remainder of cheese. Put into oven to heat through and brown lightly on top.

If preferred, chopped mushrooms which have been cooked for 5 minutes in a little butter can be added to the chicken instead of tomatoes.

## CHICKEN MADRID

Prepare chicken pieces the night before as directed in basic recipe (page 52). Next day, coat each piece of chicken in seasoned flour and brown in butter or vegetable oil until golden brown. Place in a greased casserole, cover and place in oven to heat while you make the sauce. For this you need:

| | |
|---|---|
| 4 *peeled and chopped tomatoes* | 2 *peeled and sliced onions* |
| 1 *chopped green pepper (carefully* | *butter or oil* |
| *seeded)* | *chicken stock* |
| 1 *crushed clove of garlic* | |

Fry onion and garlic in oil or butter remaining in pan from browning chicken, adding more oil if necessary. When onion is just turning golden, add tomatoes and green pepper and

54

cook for 2 or 3 minutes, crushing tomatoes into onion with a fork. Add just enough chicken stock to make a sauce, stirring until it boils, then cook together for 3 minutes. Pour over chicken in casserole, cover and cook for 20 minutes, or longer if time permits.

Serve with rice or noodles which have been cooking while the casserole heats.

Tomato paste can be used instead of tomatoes if preferred, and a spoonful of sherry or red wine improves the flavour.

## MINTED CHICKEN GRILL

Young chicken will grill to a beautiful golden tenderness in 25 to 30 minutes, and gains new flavour by being marinaded in a tasty sauce before cooking. It should be put into the marinade in the morning before leaving home, then drained and grilled in the evening. The pear-mint garnish is an unusual finish, and the marinade is thickened to make a sauce to serve with the chicken.

1 *2-lb chicken*
1 *small can of pears*
½ *cup of cider*
1 *teaspoon soya sauce*

*dash of cayenne*
2 *oz butter or oil*
2 or 3 *sprigs of fresh mint, chopped*

Cut chicken into two halves through the breastbone, trim the wing-tips and flatten chicken as much as possible. Place in a flat dish. Drain syrup from pears, add cider and soya sauce with a dash of cayenne, mix well and pour over chicken halves.

When ready to cook, drain chicken and dry, then brush liberally with melted butter or oil on both sides. Remove rack from grill pan, and arrange chicken, skin side down, in pan. Place pan 5 or 6 inches from heat, and grill gently for 10 to 12 minutes, then turn, brush over with butter or oil, and continue grilling gently for a further 12 to 15 minutes, or until joints move freely when tested. Brush over with more butter or oil while grilling.

While chicken is grilling, dice the pears and toss in a little butter until heated through and well glazed. Chop the mint leaves. Thicken the marinade with a little cornflour blended with water, stirring over low heat until thickened and smooth.

When chicken is cooked, arrange two halves on a flat serving dish, with the glazed pears sprinkled with the mint round them as a garnish. To serve, cut each half chicken into two pieces, and serve sauce separately.

## COUNTRY-STYLE CHICKEN GRILL

This is another way of grilling chicken, and needs no beforehand preparations. It is served with a mushroom sauce which is cooked while the chicken is grilling. Garnish with watercress and potato crisps. If you find it easier, 4 young chicken pieces can be used instead of the whole bird.

| | |
|---|---|
| 1 *2-lb chicken* | *salt and pepper* |
| ½ *large juicy lemon* | 2 *rashers streaky bacon, choppde* |
| 1½ *oz butter, melted* | 4 *oz mushroom caps, sliced* |

Cut chicken in halves through the breastbone, trim wingtips, and flatten chicken as much as possible. Rub pieces over with cut lemon. Melt butter in a small pan and brush over both sides of the chicken, season with salt and pepper. Remove rack from grill pan, arrange chicken pieces skinside down in pan, and grill under gentle heat for 10 or 12 minutes. Turn, brush with butter and continue grilling for a further 12 to 15 minutes, brushing over with more butter. When cooked the skin should be crisp and golden, and the joints should move freely.

56

While chicken is cooking, fry the bacon and sliced mush-rooms in butter remaining in pan for about 6 or 8 minutes, and when cooked add the lemon juice, and season lightly. A little white wine can be added to sauce if available. Serve chicken with mushroom sauce poured over it, cutting each piece in halves to make 4 servings.

## CALIFORNIA GRILL

Grill the chicken pieces as directed in previous recipe. When chicken is almost cooked, pour any remaining butter and the juices in the grill pan into a frying pan. Continue grilling the chicken.

Peel 2 bananas and cut in halves lengthwise. Finely grate enough orange rind to make 4 teaspoonfuls, and squeeze juice from the orange. Fry the bananas in the butter in frying pan, turning to brown both sides until golden. Place a banana half on each chicken joint, add orange juice to butter remaining in pan and stir to heat, then pour over chicken and banana. Sprinkle with grated rind and serve at once.

## PIQUANT CHICKEN

Cook either a boiling fowl or chicken pieces as directed on page 52. Do not overcook, as pieces must be firm. Remove skin before bird is completely cold, and cut in serving pieces if a whole bird has been cooked.

Make a thin mixture of dry mustard, a few drops of Worcestershire sauce and just enough water to blend smoothly. Using a pastry brush, brush this mustard mixture over the chicken pieces in a thin coating. Leave to dry, and put into refrigerator until ready to cook next day. Brush over with melted butter or oil, place in the grill pan without the rack, and grill under fairly quick heat until crisp and golden brown and heated through, turning to brown both sides. Do not overcook or the pieces will be dry.

Serve with French fried potatoes.

## CHICKEN AND PINEAPPLE CASSEROLE

The bland flavour of chicken combines well with pineapple in this casserole, which is prepared and cooked the night before serving, then re-heated and served with rice and fried pineapple rings as a garnish. Serve with green peas or carrot sticks.

| | |
|---|---|
| 4 *large pieces of chicken* | 1 *tablespoon sherry or lemon* |
| *seasoned flour* | *juice* |
| 2 *oz bacon fat or butter* | 1 *tablespoon butter, extra* |
| 1 *cup pineapple juice* | 4 *slices of pineapple* |
| 1 *tablespoon soya sauce* | *cooked rice* |

Coat chicken pieces in flour seasoned with salt and pepper and brown in the bacon fat or butter, turning to brown evenly on all sides. Remove from pan and place in casserole. Pour pineapple juice, soya sauce and sherry into pan and stir well until just boiling, then pour over chicken. Cover and bake in a moderate oven (350° F or No 4) for about 1¼ hours, or until chicken is tender. Cool and store in refrigerator until ready to re-heat next day, but remove from 'fridge in time to allow casserole to return to room temperature, unless a metal or enamel casserole is used.

While casserole is re-heating, cook rice, and fry pineapple slices in extra butter until browned on both sides. Serve each chicken piece on a slice of pineapple, pour gravy over the top, and surround with a ring of rice.

# CHICKEN RAYMONDE

For this delicious dish the chicken (or chicken pieces) is simmered for about 1 hour the night before serving. It is re-heated next day in the stock, and served on a bed of rice with a creamy sauce. Serve with baked halved tomatoes or green peas to provide colour to the dish.

| | |
|---|---|
| 4 *or* 5 *chicken pieces* | 3 *cups cooked rice* |
| *salt and peppercorns* | *chopped parsley* |
| *bouquet garni* | 3 *egg yolks* |
| 1 *onion stuck with* 2 *cloves* | ¼ *cup cream or evaporated milk* |
| 1 *carrot, sliced* | 3 *tablespoons grated cheese* |
| 2 *stalks of celery* | 1 *tablespoon butter* |

Put chicken into a large saucepan with bouquet garni, salt and peppercorns, onion with cloves, celery and carrot and 2 pints water. Bring to boil and simmer for 1 hour or until tender. Remove chicken pieces and carefully take off all the skin, returning skin to stock. Boil stock rapidly for 30 minutes, then strain and cool. Carefully wrap chicken pieces in foil or plastic when cold. Store chicken and stock in refrigerator until next day.

Measure ½ cup chicken stock into a saucepan and add chicken pieces, re-heating for only a few minutes. Cook the rice, and toss with chopped parsley, then place in an oven-proof dish. Arrange chicken pieces on top and keep hot. Bring 1 cup chicken stock to the boil and stir into it the egg yolk beaten with the cream, adding the grated cheese and stirring to get a smooth sauce. Pour over chicken, dot with pieces of butter and put in a hot oven or under a hot grill for a few minutes to brown until golden. Serve at once.

## CHICKEN AND ALMOND BAKE

It is worth cooking chicken pieces the night before (as directed in basic recipe, page 52), to make up this tasty dish and the ones which follow. All of them can be prepared in under 30 minutes, ready to serve. The chicken can be cut from the bone and diced or sliced in the morning if more convenient, then wrapped in foil or a plastic bag to keep from drying out in the refrigerator. The weight of chicken required is given after cutting off the bones.

| | |
|---|---|
| ¾ *lb chicken pieces* | 1 *tablespoon lemon juice* |
| 2 *cups thinly sliced celery* | 1 *cup prepared mayonnaise* |
| ½ *cup blanched, slivered almonds* | ½ *cup grated tasty cheese* |
| *salt and pepper* | 1 *cup crushed potato crisps* |
| 1 *dessertspoon grated onion* | *whole potato crisps* |

Combine chicken, celery, onion, almonds, lemon juice and mayonnaise. Turn into a greased, shallow ovenproof dish, sprinkle top with the cheese and crushed crisps mixed together. Bake in a moderate oven (350° F or No 4) for 15 to 20 minutes, until heated through and bubbling. Just before serving, remove from oven and stand a row of potato crisps around the edge of the casserole, then return to oven for a few minutes.

## CHICKEN IN THE CORN FLAN

This is a useful way of either using up left-over chicken for another tasty meal, or using chicken pieces cooked especially, to be made up like this the next day. It can be served hot or cold, and if the flan case is made and baked blind the night before, it only takes about 10 minutes to prepare. If wanted cold, the flan should be made and filled the night before, then served with a garnish of tomato slices, accompanied by a green salad.

| | |
|---|---|
| 8-inch flan case, baked blind | ½ pint chicken stock |
| ¾ lb cooked chicken, cut off the bone | 4 tablespoons cream or evaporated milk |
| 1 medium onion, chopped | 1 small can sweet corn |
| 2 oz butter or margarine | 1 tablespoon chopped parsley |
| 2 oz flour | salt and pepper |

Fry the chopped onion in the butter until transparent, but do not brown. Stir in the flour, then stir in chicken stock and continue stirring until thickened. Add cream, drained corn, chicken pieces, and parsley. Season to taste and heat for 2 or 3 minutes without boiling. Pour into flan case which has been re-heated in the oven for a few minutes. Serve at once.

If serving cold, both filling and flan case should be cooled before combining.

## CHICKEN ALEXANDRIA

All the ingredients can be prepared the night before, all ready to be put together into a casserole and baked for dinner.

| | |
|---|---|
| ¾ lb cooked chicken meat, diced | 2 oz flour |
| 4 oz cooked or canned mushrooms, sliced | ½ cup chicken stock |
| 1½ cups cooked rice | ½ cup top milk |
| 2 tablespoons chopped canned pimento | salt and pepper |
| | 1 tablespoon sherry |
| 1 tablespoon finely chopped parsley | ½ teaspoon Worcestershire sauce |
| 2 oz butter or margarine | fine buttered breadcrumbs |

If preferred, the sauce can be made just before making up the casserole. Melt butter in a saucepan, blend in flour and cook for 2 minutes, then stir in chicken stock and milk, stirring until thickened. Add sherry and Worcestershire sauce, and season to taste.

Put alternate layers of cooked rice, chicken pieces, pimento, parsley and mushrooms into a greased casserole, pour sauce over the top, then sprinkle with buttered crumbs. Bake in a hot oven (425° F or No 7) for about 10 minutes, or until mixture bubbles and is heated through.

## CHICKEN MARYLAND

This is quite quick to do if you par-boil the chicken pieces beforehand, but care should be taken not to overcook them. Do this the night before, ready for the chicken to be fried for 10 or 15 minutes before serving. Traditionally, Chicken Maryland is served with fried bananas and sweet corn, but you can please yourself, or your family, about this.

| | |
|---|---|
| *4 chicken pieces, half-cooked* | *1 egg* |
| *milk* | *soft breadcrumbs* |
| *seasoned flour* | *fat or oil for frying* |
| *4 rashers of streaky bacon* | *bananas and sweet corn* |

When ready to cook the chicken, dip the pieces in milk, then put into a paper bag with the seasoned flour and shake until well coated. Beat the egg with 1 tablespoon cold water, and dip the coated pieces first into egg mixture and then into soft breadcrumbs, pressing the crumbs in firmly. Heat enough fat or oil to give you two inches deep in a heavy frying pan, and put chicken pieces into the fat, frying until browned on all sides. Cook covered for 10 minutes, then uncover and finish cooking for 5 minutes, or until chicken is quite tender.

In another frying pan, fry the halved bacon rashers until crisp, then fry the halved, peeled bananas in bacon fat until golden brown. Heat sweet corn in own liquor, drain and add a small pat of butter. Serve chicken pieces garnished with bananas and bacon, with the sweet corn.

# FLAMING CHICKEN WITH CHERRIES

If you want to surprise some special friends with a really spectacular dish, make this one with chicken combined with black cherries, which you set alight at the table before serving. It needs no accompaniment except a tossed green salad and some crusty French bread cut in thick slices. If you have a candlewarmer, heat the Kirsch or brandy at the table over the candle, or if more convenient heat it in the kitchen and bring to the table at once, where you set it alight and pour flaming over the chickens – just as you do for your Christmas pudding. When flames have died down, serve chicken immediately.

| | |
|---|---|
| 2 2-*lb chickens or* 6 *chicken pieces* | 1 *tablespoon cornflour* |
| 1 *large can of black cherries* | 2 *tablespoons butter or oil* |
| 1 *cup claret or burgundy* | *salt and pepper* |
| ¼ *cup cherry juice* | *wine glass of Kirsch or brandy* |

Cook chickens or chicken pieces as directed on page 52. If whole birds are used, cut them into serving pieces. Cover and store in refrigerator until ready to finish cooking. Then heat butter or oil in thick frying pan and fry chicken on all sides, seasoning with salt and pepper, until golden and heated through.

While chicken is frying, make the cherry sauce. Heat the stoned cherries in the wine, blend cornflour with cherry juice and stir into cherries, stirring until thick and clear. When chicken is golden and heated through, pour cherry sauce round it and bring to the boil, then pour immediately into a heated ovenproof serving dish and cover to bring to the table,

Put Kirsch or brandy into a metal ladle and heat over candle-warmer, set alight and quickly pour over chicken. Serve at once, for 6.

## CHICKEN AND HAM POTPIE

Instead of pastry, this pie has a topping of scone dough, made from the ready-blend mix given on page 170, which is baked while the chicken and ham filling is heating. As all the main ingredients for the filling are cooked the night before, this delicious pie can be prepared and cooked in 30 minutes. Serve it with halved tomatoes baked in the oven at the same time as the topping. The chicken meat can be stripped from the bones after cooking, or it can be left as whole pieces.

4 or 5 *chicken pieces, cooked*  
6 *oz chopped, cooked ham*  
½ *cup cooked peas*  
½ *cup mixed, diced cooked carrots and celery*

1 *oz butter or margarine*  
1 *oz flour*  
*salt and pepper*  
½ *pint milk*  
¼ *pint chicken stock*

FOR THE TOPPING  
8 *oz ready-blend flour mix*  
1 *teaspoon grated onion*

½ *teaspoon mixed dried herbs*  
*not quite ¼ pint milk*

Mix the ready-blend flour mix with herbs, onion and just enough milk to make a soft dough. Turn out on a lightly floured board and press into a round the same size as the casserole in which pie is to be heated. (Turn casserole upside down and mark dough.) Place on a floured baking sheet, and bake in a hot oven (450° F or No 8) for 15 to 20 minutes. The top may be brushed over with milk or lightly beaten egg yolk to glaze.

While the topping is baking, make the sauce by melting the butter or margarine in a saucepan, then blending in the flour, and cooking for 2 minutes. Slowly stir in milk and chicken stock, and continue stirring until sauce thickens. Cook for 2 or 3 minutes, then add cooked vegetables, ham and chicken and re-heat for a few minutes. Turn into greased casserole, cover and put into bottom of oven until topping is cooked. Bake tomato halves at the same time.

To serve, place baked topping on the top of chicken in casserole and bring to table. Cut in wedges, to serve 4 or 5.

# CURRIED CHICKEN CASSEROLE

You can make this curry as mild or as hot as your taste dictates, but if the curry sauce is made the night before, remember when re-heating that the curry flavour usually strengthens if allowed to stand overnight. Serve the curry with as many garnishes as you can manage, all of which can be prepared the night before. These can include crisply cooked bacon crumbled into pieces, chopped hard-boiled eggs, chopped peanuts or hazelnuts, lemon wedges, chutney, seedless raisins plumped in hot water and dried, and grated coconut. Choose which garnishes you want to serve, and put each one in a small dish, then put all the small dishes on a large dish or tray to make it easy to pass round. If you have one of those sectioned hors d'oeuvre dishes, use it to serve your curry garnishes. Bananas baked in the oven in a little butter make a nice accompaniment to the curry, instead of a vegetable, and of course, a dish of fluffy rice is essential.

4 *or* 5 *pieces of pre-cooked chicken*
1½ *oz butter or chicken fat*
1½ *oz flour*
1 *clove of garlic* (optional)
1 *small onion, finely chopped*

1 *cooking apple*
1 *tablespoon curry powder or to taste*
2 *cups chicken stock*
*salt and pepper*
*cooked rice*

C

Brown the chicken pieces in the hot fat with the garlic, turning to brown on all sides until golden. Remove with a slotted spoon, drain on paper and place in a greased casserole. Cover and place in a moderate oven (350° F or No 4) to keep hot while sauce is being made, and rice cooked.

Remove garlic from pan and add chopped onion and chopped and peeled apple to fat in pan, frying gently until onions are soft. Push to one side and blend in flour and curry powder, cook for 2 minutes, then stir in stock. Continue stirring until sauce thickens and boils, then simmer gently for 5 minutes, stirring occasionally. Taste for seasoning and pour over chicken in casserole. Continue cooking for 15 to 20 minutes, when mixture should be bubbling. Serve with rice and assorted garnishes.

## CHINESE CHICKEN AND ALMONDS

If you have enjoyed this dish in a Chinese restaurant, you will know how delicious it is, served with cooked rice or noodles. Here is a very simple recipe for the dish, which can be made up in under half an hour if all preparations have been done beforehand. The rice or noodles are cooked while the sauce is made.

¾ *lb cooked chicken meat, diced*
*bunch of spring onions, or 1 small*
*   onion, sliced*
4 *oz mushrooms, sliced thin*
2 *oz blanched almonds*
2 *tablespoons cooked green beans*
*   or peas*

*fat or oil for frying*
½ *oz cornflour*
4 *tablespoons chicken stock*
1 *teaspoon soya sauce*
*salt and pepper*

Fry the blanched almonds in a little hot oil or fat until lightly browned and crisp. Remove from fat and drain on paper. In the same pan, adding a little more oil or fat, fry the sliced onions and mushrooms, stirring well with a fork, then add chicken pieces and stock, and cook for a few minutes until just boiling. Stir in cornflour which has been blended with a little stock and sauce, and stir until thickened. Simmer for a few minutes, stirring carefully not to break up chicken pieces too much. Add vegetables and when hot, serve the chicken mixture over the cooked rice or noodles. Sprinkle almonds over the top and serve at once.

## CHINESE FRIED CHICKEN

The sweet-sour marinade used for this recipe gives a distinctive flavour to the chicken, which is cooked and prepared the night before, then fried for 5 or 6 minutes just before serving. Cook chicken or chicken pieces as directed on page 52, then drain and dry, adding to the marinade while still warm, and leaving overnight. In the morning, turn the chicken pieces in the marinade.

| | |
|---|---|
| 4 *cooked chicken pieces* | 1 *cup water* |
| ½ *cup honey* | ¾ *cup flour* |
| ¼ *cup vinegar* | *dash of pepper* |
| ½ *cup soya sauce* | *vegetable oil* |

Make marinade with warmed honey, vinegar, soya sauce and water, mixing well. Arrange chicken pieces in a shallow dish and pour marinade over them. Set aside overnight, remembering to turn the pieces in the marinade in the morning before leaving home.

When ready to cook, drain the chicken. Put flour and pepper in a bag and toss chicken pieces in flour until well coated. Heat oil in a large frying pan and fry chicken until golden brown and crisp on both sides. Drain on paper and serve at once. The marinade can be thickened with a little cornflour and served as a sauce with the chicken if liked.

# CHINESE FRIED RICE WITH CHICKEN

Rice and chicken are natural affinities, and many countries have their own versions of the popular combination. This Chinese one is very tasty, and although left-over chicken can be used, it is worth cooking some chicken pieces especially to make this dish. Left-over turkey or duck pieces can also be given new flavours when made up like this. The rice and chicken can be cooked the night before, also the omelette if necessary. Have all the ingredients prepared before you start cooking the dish, as it needs almost constant attention while it is being cooked, which only takes about 20 minutes.

| | |
|---|---|
| 2 *eggs* | 8 *oz cold, cooked chicken, diced* |
| 2 *teaspoons butter* | 2 *or* 3 *oz cooked ham, shredded* |
| *salt and pepper* | 2 *oz mushrooms, sliced thin* |
| 4 *tablespoons vegetable oil* | 1 *stalk of celery, sliced thin* |
| 4 *cups cold, cooked rice* | 2 *oz cooked shrimps, sliced* |
| ½ *cup cooked peas* | 2 *teaspoons soya sauce* |
| 1 *small onion, chopped* | |

Beat the eggs with salt and pepper and 1 tablespoon of cold water. Heat butter in a small pan, swirling round to grease the bottom and sides of pan, then pour in the egg mixture, and cook over low heat until set on the bottom. Put under a pre-heated grill until top is set, and mixture is fairly firm. This can be made the night before if more convenient, cooled, wrapped in foil and stored in 'fridge until ready to fry the rice.

Using a fairly large, thick pan, heat 2 tablespoons oil and add ½ teaspoon salt. When it is very hot add the rice and sauté for 5 minutes, turning frequently with a fork. Remove from pan and keep warm. Add remaining oil to pan and brown the onion until golden. Add mushrooms and celery and cook for 2 minutes, turning frequently, then slowly stir in rice and remainder of ingredients, mixing well, lastly adding the omelette cut into ¼-inch strips. When mixture is heated through, turn into four shallow bowls and serve at once.

## CHICKEN AND RICE LOAF

Make this the night before, store in refrigerator when cold, and serve cold next day for dinner with crisp lettuce leaves, sliced tomatoes and cucumber. This is also a good dish to take for a picnic, as it can be carried in the tin in which it was baked, then cut in slices to serve with bread and butter and a salad such as lettuce, carrot strips and small, whole tomatoes which can be eaten in the fingers. These amounts serve 6 or 7.

| | |
|---|---|
| 3½ *to* 4 *lb boiling fowl* | 1½ *cups cooked rice* |
| 4 *medium-size carrots* | 2 *eggs, slightly beaten* |
| 3 *stalks of celery, with leaves* | 1 *sweet red pepper or canned* |
| *salt and pepper* | *pimento, chopped* |

Cook bird as directed on page 52, cool and cut meat from the bones. Put chicken meat, carrots and celery through the fine blade of your mincer, add rice and beaten eggs, red pepper or pimento, and season to taste. Mix all very well together and turn into a greased loaf tin or oblong ovenproof dish. If mixture seems too dry, add a little chicken stock. Bake in a moderate oven (375° F or No 5) for 45 to 50 minutes, or until firm and browned on top. Test with a clean knifeblade to see if loaf is cooked through. Cool in tin.

If you have the required time for cooking, this loaf can also be served hot, with some of the stock thickened to make a sauce.

## CHICKEN AND RICE MEDLEY

This makes a very good cold meal for a warm day, served with crisp lettuce, sliced tomatoes and cucumber. The rice mixture is prepared the night before and stored in a covered bowl in the refrigerator. Either left-over chicken can be used, or chicken pieces cooked the night before and stored in 'fridge until ready to serve. The meat is then cut from the bones into chunks, and tossed with the rice mixture just before serving. Mayonnaise is served separately.

| | |
|---|---|
| 2 *cups diced cooked chicken meat* | 1 *tablespoon chopped parsley* |
| 2 *cups cold, cooked rice* | ½ *cup grated raw carrot* |
| 1 *cup diced celery* | *French dressing* (page 148) |
| 1 *sweet red pepper, chopped* | *salt and pepper* |
| 1 *tablespoon grated onion* | *mayonnaise* |

Mix the rice and prepared vegetables, and add just enough French dressing to moisten lightly, but do not make mixture soggy. Toss well together, seasoning with salt and pepper if necessary, and store in 'fridge until ready to serve. Complete as given above.

This looks nice arranged in individual serves on lettuce leaves, and garnished with tomato and cucumber slices.

## TERRINE OF CHICKEN

A dish for a buffet party, served cold with salad, or as a first course for dinner with fingers of freshly made toast. It is made the night before serving, and allowed to get cold in the dish in which it was cooked, then turned out when ready to serve. It will take some time to prepare and cook, so give yourself a free evening for the job, but it is well worth it.

| | |
|---|---|
| 3½ *to* 4 *lb chicken* | *salt and black pepper* |
| 1 *chicken liver* | 1 *tablespoon finely chopped* |
| ¾ *lb pork sausage meat* | *parsley* |
| 1 *small onion* | 1 *beaten egg* |
| *finely grated rind* ½ *lemon* | 6 *to* 8 *strips fat pork or bacon* |

With a sharp knife remove the breasts of the chicken, and cut into long thin strips. Cut remaining flesh from the bones, and put through the fine blade of the mincer with the chicken liver and peeled onion, and lastly the sausage meat. Add lemon rind, chopped parsley and season to taste, then bind mixture with beaten egg, mixing all very well together. Using a deep oblong ovenproof dish or loaf tin, line the bottom with strips of fat bacon or pork. Press in a thick layer of the minced mixture, then arrange slices of chicken breast over the top, with a piece of fat bacon. Repeat these layers, pressing each down until dish is filled, and all ingredients are used, finishing with a layer of fat bacon. Cover with foil, and stand dish in a baking tin with water coming half-way up the sides of the dish. Bake in a moderate oven (350° F or No 4) for about 2 hours. Gives 8 to 10 small serves.

## ASPARAGUS AND CHICKEN ASPIC

A recipe for a summer dinner, with the happy alliance of asparagus and chicken set in jelly, ready to be turned out and served with a colourful salad. Make this the night before it is to be served.

2 *cups cooked, diced chicken*
½ *pint chicken stock, strained*
2 *tablespoons tarragon vinegar*
1 *tablespoon brandy*
¼ *cup cold water*

¾ *oz gelatine*
1 *large can asparagus tips*
*salt and pepper*
*mayonnaise*
*lettuce, tomatoes, cooked peas*

Soften gelatine in cold water. Bring stock and vinegar to the boil, remove from heat and stir in gelatine until dissolved. Add brandy, salt and pepper, and cool slightly. Pour a little of the gelatine mixture into the bottom of an oblong mould, put into refrigerator until nearly set. Arrange half the well-drained asparagus tips in a neat layer and cover with aspic, then chill until set. Put chicken in a layer over the asparagus, cover with aspic and chill until set, then cover with remaining layer of asparagus and more aspic. Chill until ready to serve.

Unmould on a cold serving dish, surround with crisp lettuce leaves, with a spoonful of cold cooked peas in each leaf, and garnish with sliced tomatoes. Cut mould in slices, and serve mayonnaise separately.

## COLD CHICKEN IN SHERRY SAUCE

This is a dinner-party dish when you want to serve something cold. The chicken is cooked the night before (see page 52) and left in the stock until cool. In the morning before leaving home, cut chicken into serving pieces (it may be cut from the bones if preferred) and arrange on a serving plate. Make the sauce and pour over chicken pieces, coating each one, then put aside in a cool larder, or in refrigerator, until ready to serve. Garnish with asparagus tips tied into bundles of three or four with strips of canned pimento.

| | |
|---|---|
| 1 *cooked 4-lb chicken* | 1 *pint cream* |
| 6 *egg yolks* | *finely grated rind of lemon* |
| 2 *wineglasses of sherry* | *canned asparagus tips* |
| | *pimento strips* |

Make the sauce by heating cream in top of a double saucepan over hot water. Add sherry and well-beaten egg yolks, and stir lightly until thickened. Remove from heat. Pour over chicken pieces, and sprinkle lemon rind over top as a garnish. Cool until ready to serve. For 6.

# DUCK AU CITRON

Ducks are fatty birds, and need an accompaniment which will counteract the fatty taste. Fruits of various kinds are used for this, and there are many recipes combining duck with prunes as in Denmark, with cherries as they do in France, or with oranges as they do in Spain.

In this recipe the duck is cooked first as in the basic recipe for chicken on page 52. It is then cooled and wrapped in foil or plastic and stored in refrigerator until next night, when the last stage of the cooking is done before serving. The duck can be left whole or cut in pieces for the last stage of cooking, as desired.

| | |
|---|---|
| cooked duck | 2 cups stock from duck |
| seasoned flour | 3 tablespoons orange marmalade |
| pinch ground ginger | 1 cup orange juice |
| 1 small onion | 4 or 5 orange shells |
| fat or vegetable oil | cooked peas |

Rub the duck over with seasoned flour to which you have added the ground ginger, then brown in hot fat or oil, turning to brown evenly all over. Remove from pan and place in greased casserole. Brown the sliced onion in fat in pan, then pour off any surplus fat, and blend 2 tablespoons flour into pan, scraping up any residue from the pan. Stir in stock and blend well, then add orange juice and stir until thick and boiling. Stir in marmalade.

Pour marmalade sauce over duck in casserole, cover and bake in a well heated, moderately hot oven (375° F or No 5) for 25 to 30 minutes.

Serve the hot, cooked peas in scooped-out orange halves which have been warmed in the oven. Potato crisps are good with this dish, which serves 4 or 5, depending on size of duck.

## HAWAIIAN DUCK

In this recipe pineapple juice and pineapple slices as a garnish are a good accompaniment to the duck. The bird is cooked as in the basic recipe (page 52), then cut in pieces, cooled and stored in refrigerator until ready to re-heat next day.

2½ to 3 *lb duck, cooked*  2 *stalks celery, sliced thin*
¼ *cup soya sauce*  1 *cup pineapple juice*
1 *tablespoon sugar*  1 *cup duck stock*
1 *teaspoon ground ginger*  *cornflour*
*seasoned flour*  *pineapple slices*
*fat or vegetable oil*

Mix sauce, sugar and ground ginger and dip duck pieces into mixture, coating well. Then coat with seasoned flour and brown all over in hot oil or fat. Remove to a greased casserole, and cook sliced celery in the oil for a few minutes, then add to duck in casserole. Combine stock and pineapple juice, heat, and pour over duck. Cover and bake in a fairly hot oven (400° F or No 6) for 25 to 30 minutes. The gravy in the casserole may be thickened with a little cornflour if desired.

Fry pineapple slices in oil remaining in pan, turning to brown lightly both sides. Serve a portion of duck on each pineapple slice and pour sauce over. This is usually served with cooked rice.

# TURKEY AND MUSHROOM PIE

This is a good way to use up the left-overs from a large turkey, and it gives the bird a new flavour in case the family are tired of turkey, especially after Christmas. Remove every scrap of meat from the carcase with a small, sharp knife. Break up the bones, put into a saucepan with an onion, 1 small carrot, and some celery leaves, salt, pepper and a bay leaf and barely cover with water. Bring to the boil, then simmer for at least an hour, tightly covered. Strain and put stock aside to cool. Peel 2 lb potatoes and cook until tender, then drain away all but 2 tablespoons of the water in which they were cooked. Add 1 tablespoon of butter to the potatoes, season to taste and mash until smooth and creamy. Turn into a bowl when quite cold, cover with foil and leave in a cool larder until next day. When ready to use as cover for the pie, stand the bowl of potatoes over a saucepan of boiling water until warmed through, then beat lightly with a fork to make them malleable. For the pie you need:

| | |
|---|---|
| *turkey pieces (at least 2 cupfuls)* | *2 tablespoons butter or bacon fat* |
| *2 large onions, chopped* | *1½ oz flour* |
| *4 oz mushrooms, sliced* | *2 cups turkey stock* |
| *2 sticks celery, chopped* | *salt and pepper* |
| | *½ cup grated cheese* |

When ready to cook pie, melt fat in a thick pan and sauté the onion until transparent, then add celery and mushrooms and continue cooking for 5 minutes, stirring with a fork to cook evenly. Push vegetables to one side and blend in flour, cooking for a minute, then stir in stock, and cook until thickened. Add turkey pieces and season to taste. Grease an ovenproof pie dish or casserole and turn turkey mixture into it. Cover with a topping of mashed potatoes, and sprinkle with grated cheese. Put into a moderate oven (375° F or No 5) until topping is golden and crisp, then serve at once.

# Meat Dishes

Few people can afford often to buy best quality steak and chops for grilling in order to enjoy easily prepared meals – and I think you would get rather tired of them day after day. Luckily the business woman who must rush home to prepare a meal for her family, or serve a good dinner to guests in only a short time, can find many ways of cooking and serving the less-expensive cuts of meat.

With careful preparation and planning, there are few dishes which cannot be served up in half an hour after Madame returns home – but she must have made her preparations in advance.

Most stews and casseroles improve with being made the night before and re-heated just before serving, but care must be taken not to overcook the meat or it loses much of its flavour and nourishment. To my mind roasted meats do not re-heat successfully, so save your roast for the week-end when you can spend time in cooking it to a crisp brown succulence.

If a meat loaf takes too much time to cook, make small individual loaves which will bake in 30 minutes, while the vegetables and potatoes are cooking.

When the family tire of casseroles give them Cheesed Beef-burgers (page 89) which can be prepared in advance and only need 12 minutes to cook. Or a Steak Plate-pie (page 85) which cooks in 30 minutes if you have done your preparations the night before, or Meat Loaves with Spaghetti (page 89).

The cheaper cuts of meat have just as high nutritive value as the more expensive cuts (such as rump or fillet steak) but they need long, slow cooking to make them tender.

They can be simmered, braised or casseroled, or a pressure

cooker is very useful for cooking those tougher cuts to best advantage. Many cheaper cuts of meat may be tenderized and improved in flavour by leaving in a marinade (page 110) for some hours before cooking. This can usually be done in the morning before leaving home, and the meat is then ready to cook in the evening.

If you have prepared a stew or casserole just large enough for the family, and an unexpected guest arrives home with your husband, don't despair; just make up some dumplings or use some of the ready-mixed scone dough you have in the refrigerator (page 170) and you will find the prepared dish will stretch to another serve. Rice is another good 'stretcher' for a stew which has plenty of good rich gravy, and this is easily increased by adding a beef cube and some extra water to the pot. Cook the rice separately, add some chopped parsley, and serve in a ring round the stew. Nobody will ever know it was 'stretched' and it will taste just as good.

## BRAISED BEEF ROLLS

A tasty version of the old favourite, beef-olives, given added flavour with mushrooms and red wine for a special dish.

1½ *lb topside steak*
1½ *cups chopped vegetables*
3 *rashers lean bacon*
*salt and pepper*
*plain flour*
*beef dripping or oil*

½ *lb peeled, chopped tomatoes or*
  1 *small can tomatoes*
4 *oz mushrooms*
*red wine if desired*
1 *bay leaf*

Ask your butcher to cut the steak into slices about ¼-inch thick. Cut into 4-inch squares, pounding the meat as thin as possible without breaking it, using the back of a wooden spoon if you haven't got a meat mallet. The mixed vegetables should include finely chopped carrot, celery, onion, and parsley, seasoned with salt and pepper. Chop the bacon very small and mix with vegetables. Place a spoonful of this mixture on each square of steak, then roll up like a parcel, tucking the ends in securely. Tie with white thread. Roll in seasoned flour, heat fat or oil in saucepan and brown rolls on all sides, browning only two or three at one time, and removing when browned all over. Pour off any fat remaining in pan and arrange rolls in a single layer, if possible, in saucepan. Add tomatoes and bay leaf and 4 cups water and bring to boil, then cover and simmer gently for 2 hours, or until beef is tender. Remove rolls with a slotted spoon, cool and store in refrigerator. Strain off liquor in pan, cool and store in refrigerator separately.

When ready to cook next day, wash and slice mushrooms and cook in a little oil for 5 minutes, stirring occasionally. Blend 2 tablespoons flour into oil remaining in pan then pour in gravy from rolls and stir until mixture boils and thickens. Place beef rolls in gravy and re-heat, adding about ½ cup wine if using.

Serve with fluffy mashed potatoes.

## BEEF CASSEROLE MILANO

A crusty topping of macaroni and cheese is an unusual feature of this dish, which is first cooked on top of the stove in a saucepan, and then transferred to a casserole to finish cooking just before serving. To serve 4 or 5.

1½ *lb stewing steak*
1 *large onion, sliced*
1 *bay leaf*
1 *clove of garlic, if liked*
2 *whole cloves*
*salt and peppercorns*

½ *lb tomatoes, peeled* or 1 *tablespoon tomato paste*
2 *cups diced celery*
1 *large carrot, sliced*
6 *oz macaroni*
2 *cups grated tasty cheese*

Cut beef into cubes, removing any fat. Put into a saucepan

78

with the bay leaf, cloves, onion, crushed garlic if using, salt and whole peppercorns, and cover with cold water. Bring to the boil, skim if necessary, then cover and simmer for $1\frac{1}{2}$ hours or longer, until meat is tender. Add the prepared vegetables for the last 30 minutes cooking time.

Drain off broth from the saucepan, and arrange meat and vegetables in an ovenproof dish. When cold, cover and store in 'fridge until next day. Cool and store broth in 'fridge also. Next night, cook macaroni in boiling salted water until tender, about 12 to 15 minutes, then drain well. While macaroni is cooking, place meat and vegetables in casserole in the oven to warm through. Heat the broth. Arrange the drained macaroni in a layer over the meat and vegetables, add just enough broth to cover meat (but not macaroni), sprinkle with cheese and bake in a hot oven until topping is golden and cheese has formed a crisp top. Serve at once.

## SPANISH BEEF CASSEROLE

A casserole which re-heats up to a rich tenderness after its initial cooking the night before is always a boon to the busy woman, and this one is recommended. It should be cooked for $1\frac{1}{2}$ hours the night before, then re-heated for about 20 minutes before serving. Cook celery hearts as a vegetable for this while casserole is re-heating.

1 *lb stewing steak*
*flour*
*salt, pepper and dry mustard*
*fat or vegetable oil*
1 *clove of garlic, if liked*

1 *bay leaf*
2 *large onions, sliced thin*
1 *small green pepper, sliced*
$\frac{1}{2}$ *lb peeled tomatoes, sliced*

Cut steak into squares. Toss in a paper bag with flour seasoned with salt, pepper and mustard. Heat fat in pan and brown the garlic if using, then remove and cook the onions for a few minutes, turning often with a fork to brown lightly.

Remove from pan and put half the onions into a greased casserole. Brown meat in pan, adding a little more fat if necessary, and turn meat to brown on all sides. Remove from pan and put half the meat over the onion layer, add sliced pepper and tomatoes, remainder of meat, then finish with a layer of onions, seasoning each layer as necessary.

Pour 2 cups of water into pan in which steak was browned, and bring to quick, rolling boil to loosen the crust on the bottom of pan. Strain over the meat in the casserole. Cover and cook in a moderate oven for $1\frac{1}{2}$ hours, or until meat is tender. Uncover and allow to cool slightly, then pour off gravy from casserole, and store in a covered basin in refrigerator when cold. Cover casserole when cold and store in 'fridge.

Next day, remove casserole from 'fridge as soon as you return home. Heat the gravy, and thicken with flour blended with a little water, stirring until it boils and thickens. Pour over the casserole, then put into a moderately hot oven until heated through and bubbling hot.

## COUNTRY-STYLE OX TAIL

Ox tail makes a good rich stew, which improves with re-heating. The vegetables are cooked in with the ox tail when it is re-heated, and instead of potatoes you can add dumplings to the gravy (see page 171). An extra green vegetable can be served if desired, and for a richer flavour add $\frac{1}{2}$ cup red wine.

| | |
|---|---|
| 1 *ox tail, cut into joints* | *salt and pepper* |
| 1 *medium onion, sliced* | 4 *small onions, peeled* |
| 2 *tablespoons plain flour* | 2 *carrots, quartered* |
| *salt and pepper* | 6 *potatoes, peeled* |
| 1 *tablespoon dripping or oil* | 1 *lb tomatoes* or 1 *medium can* |
| 1 *bay leaf* | *of tomatoes* |
| $\frac{1}{4}$ *teaspoon mixed herbs* | *chopped parsley* |
| 1 *beef cube* | 2 *cups hot water* |

Toss joints of ox tail in flour seasoned with salt and pepper.
Heat dripping or oil and brown meat on all sides. Add
onions, tomatoes, herbs, bay leaf, seasonings and hot water
and bring to boil. Cover and simmer gently for 2 to 2½ hours,
or until meat is tender. Cool, turn into bowl and store in
refrigerator until ready to re-heat. (Remove bay leaf.)

When ready to re-heat, carefully skim fat from surface,
and turn meat and gravy into a saucepan. Bring to boiling
point, and add prepared vegetables, simmering until vegetables are tender, about 20 minutes. Stir in beef cube and
wine if using, and if necessary thicken gravy with remainder
of flour, blended with a little water. Sprinkle with parsley
and serve at once.

## SAVOURY OX TAIL

This dish is cooked for about 2 hours the night before, then
cooled and stored in refrigerator. Before re-heating, the fat
is skimmed from the top, and the meat and vegetables
brought just to boiling point in a saucepan. If preferred, the
meat can be stripped from the bones before re-heating, and
the gravy thickened with a little cornflour. Any gravy left
over makes a good base for soup next day.

I sometimes turn the re-heated mixture into a pie dish and
cover with a topping as given on page 64, for Chicken and
Ham Potpie. Or drop herb dumplings into the saucepan
when it comes to the boil, and cook for 25 minutes (page 171).

| | |
|---|---|
| 1 *ox tail, cut into joints* | *bouquet garni* |
| 1 *tablespoon fat* | 1 *small green pepper* |
| 2 *rashers of bacon, diced* | 4 *whole carrots* |
| 2 *large onions, sliced* | 1 *parsnip, sliced* |
| 3 *stalks of celery, sliced* | *salt and pepper to taste* |
| 1 *clove of garlic, crushed* | *cornflour* |

Heat fat in saucepan and cook bacon for a few minutes, then remove. Add ox tail joints to hot fat and brown on all sides, then remove while you fry the onion until slightly browned, stirring with a fork to brown evenly. Pour off any surplus fat, replace ox tail and bacon and add all other ingredients, except cornflour. Add just enough hot water to well cover the meat and vegetables. Cover and bring to the boil, then simmer for about 2 hours, or until meat is quite tender. Turn into a bowl and when cold, store, covered, in refrigerator until ready to re-heat. Remove bouquet garni.

## BOEUF STROGANOFF

Another recipe for a special occasion, such as when your husband asks somebody important home for dinner, and fortunately you have a good piece of fillet steak in the refrigerator. The whole dish will take about 10 minutes to prepare and no more than 20 minutes to cook. Instead of potatoes, serve with egg-noodles tossed lightly in butter and a green salad.

| | |
|---|---|
| 1½ *lb fillet steak* | 2 *oz butter* |
| 3 *medium sized onions* | *salt and pepper* |
| ½ *lb button mushrooms* | ¼ *pint sour cream* |
| 1 *dessertspoon tomato paste* | 1 *teaspoon flour* |

The steak should be sliced about ½-inch thick, then cut into strips about 2 inches long. Peel and slice onion as thin as possible. Wash and slice mushrooms evenly, cutting through the stem to the crown to get a nice shape. Heat half the butter in a deep frying pan and cook the onions until soft and transparent, turning to cook evenly. Add mushrooms and cook for 2 minutes with the onions, then remove from pan. Add remainder of butter, heat until frothing, then add steak and fry quickly for 3 or 4 minutes. Replace onions and mushrooms, season to taste and cook together for a minute. Blend tomato paste and flour into sour cream and stir into pan with steak, increasing heat slightly. Simmer gently for 2 minutes, then serve at once.

## STEAK DIANE

A tender grilled steak is always acceptable for dinner, but just in case you would like to 'dress up' your steak, here are some recipes to make a good steak even better, starting with this very simple one. Cooking time is about 5 minutes.

Allow ¼ lb fillet or rump steak for each serve, and do not attempt to cook more than 4 steaks at once. Remove any fat from steaks, and pound each one until about ¼-inch thick, using a meat mallet or the back of a wooden spoon.

| | |
|---|---|
| 4 *pieces of grilling steak* | 1 *clove of garlic* |
| 1 *heaped tablespoon finely chopped* | 3 *oz butter* |
| *parsley* | 1 *teaspoon Worcestershire sauce* |
| *salt and freshly ground black pepper* | |

Use a good thick frying pan large enough to take all four steaks at once. If this is not available, cook two at a time in a smaller pan. Rub each steak well on both sides with salt and pepper. If you have a garlic press, extract the juice from the garlic and mix with parsley; or crush garlic well and mix with parsley. Heat 2 oz of butter in pan until it sizzles, then drop in the steaks, shaking the pan quickly to prevent them sticking. Cook quickly for 1 minute, then turn steaks over. Sprinkle them with half the parsley-garlic mixture, cook 1 minute and turn over again. Sprinkle other side with remainder of parsley-garlic mixture, and with the sauce. Shake pan well, remove steaks to heated plates and add remainder of butter to pan, swirling it round in the juices, then pour over the steaks. Serve at once with potato crisps.

## STEAK AU POIVRE

Here is a recipe for a special occasion, or for when you feel extravagant and your butcher has just told you he has a nice tender piece of fillet steak he can heartily recommend.

But although it is special it is very simple to prepare and cook, and should not take more than 10 minutes. Serve with French fried potatoes and a tossed green salad, and perhaps halved, grilled tomatoes if you want a vegetable.

| | |
|---|---|
| 1½ *to* 2 *lb fillet steak, cut thick* | 1 *teaspoon oil* |
| *freshly ground pepper* | ¼ *pint dry white wine* |
| 1 *oz butter* | 1 *teaspoon butter, extra* |

Using a pepper grinder set to coarse grind, sprinkle the steak liberally on both sides with the coarse pepper, and pound it firmly into the steak with the back of a wooden spoon.

Heat the oil and 1 oz butter in a thick pan and brown the steak on both sides very quickly to keep it rare. Remove to a heated plate and keep warm. Stir the wine into the juices in pan and simmer for 3 minutes. Add teaspoon of butter and pour over steak. Serve at once.

## CANTON BEEF

This is a well-flavoured beef dish which improves by being re-heated next day. Serve it with rice, and garnish with lemon wedges dipped into chopped parsley.

| | |
|---|---|
| 1 *lb topside steak* | 2 *teaspoons curry powder* |
| 1 *tablespoon flour* | 1 *teaspoon soya sauce* |
| *salt and pepper* | 1 *teaspoon vinegar* |
| 1 *tablespoon oil* | *good pinch cayenne* |
| 2 *large onions, sliced thin* | 2 *cups water* |
| 1 *small green pepper, sliced* | ½ *cup rice* |
| 1 *cooking apple, chopped* | 2 *tablespoons sultanas* |

Cut meat into 1-inch strips and roll in flour seasoned with salt and pepper. Heat oil in large saucepan and fry onions and green pepper (celery may be used instead of green pepper if preferred) for a few minutes, then add meat and brown well. Stir in curry powder, then add soya sauce, vinegar, apple, cayenne and water and bring to boil. Cover and simmer gently for $1\frac{1}{2}$ hours, or until meat is tender. Cool and turn mixture into a covered basin and store in refrigerator until next day.

When ready to cook, wash rice well and add to a saucepan of fast boiling water, with some salt. Cook for 12 minutes, until rice is tender, then drain and run hot water through the rice. Keep hot over boiling water. While rice is cooking re-heat the beef in a saucepan, stirring at intervals. Pour boiling water over sultanas and stand for a few minutes, then drain, and toss with rice. Serve in a ring round the Beef Canton.

## STEAK PLATE-PIE

The meat and mushroom filling for this pie is prepared the night before, then cooled and stored in the refrigerator. The pastry can also be made up the night before and stored (well wrapped in foil or a plastic bag) with the meat filling, or you can use ready-prepared frozen pastry bought from your local store.

It will only take a few minutes to roll out the pastry and make up the pie, which requires 25 to 30 minutes baking in a hot oven. Mashed potatoes and vegetables can cook while the pie is baking.

$\frac{3}{4}$ *lb short pastry*
2 *large onions, sliced*
1 *lb chuck steak*
2 *oz fat*

2 *tablespoons flour*
4 *oz mushrooms, peeled and sliced*
$\frac{1}{2}$ *pint stock or water*
*salt and pepper*

Sauté onions in fat until pale golden. Cut meat into cubes and toss in the flour seasoned with salt and pepper, then fry in the same pan, turning to brown on all sides. Add mushrooms and stock, bring to boil and simmer, covered, for $1\frac{1}{2}$ hours or until meat is tender. Allow to cool, then store in refrigerator, covered.

When ready to cook dinner, roll out the pastry, dividing into two portions, one slightly larger than the other. Use the smaller portion to line a lightly greased 8-inch pie plate, and roll remainder into a 10-inch round.

Pile the cold meat filling into the centre of lined plate, moisten edges of pastry with water and cover with other pastry round. Seal edges together firmly, trim off surplus edge, and crimp firmly. Make two slits in the top, and brush over with milk or beaten egg. Bake in centre of a hot oven (425° F or No 7) for 25 to 30 minutes, until pastry is golden brown. Serve at once.

## CROUSTADE OF SAVOURY MINCE

A croustade is a case made with mashed potato and then baked as a container for many different varieties of foods, usually prepared in a sauce. The croustade can be prepared the night before, then baked just before filling, and it is a good idea when serving mashed potatoes to make double quantities for a croustade next day. In this recipe the filling is made with minced steak, either bought already minced, or put through the mincer at home. This can also be cooked the night before and re-heated, but it only takes 30 minutes cooking time, so the mince could be cooked just before serving, if the other ingredients are left ready prepared.

FOR THE CROUSTADE
3 *cups smoothly mashed potato*      1 *beaten egg*
1 *dessertspoon melted butter*          *salt and pepper*

FOR THE MINCE

| | |
|---|---|
| ½ *lb minced steak* | *salt and pepper* |
| 1 *large onion, finely chopped* | 1 *tablespoon tomato paste* |
| 1 *stalk of celery, chopped small* | 2 *tablespoons flour* |
| 1 *sweet red pepper, shredded (if* | *stock (made with bouillon cube if* |
| *obtainable)* | *necessary)* |
| ½ *teaspoon dry mustard* | 1 *tablespoon chopped parsley* |
| 1 *dessertspoon fat* | |

Use a 6- or 7-inch cake tin for the croustade, preferably one with a loose base, and grease it well. If the potato has been cooked and mashed the night before, revive it in a basin over hot water until pliable. When mashing the night before, do not add butter, just a little milk or a little of the potato water to get a smooth consistency. When potato is warmed through beat in the melted butter and just enough beaten egg to get a smooth mixture, but do not make it too moist. Line the sides and bottom of the cake tin with the potato mixture, smoothing it round evenly. Bake in a fairly hot oven (425° F or No 7) until golden brown and crisp, then carefully remove from tin and place on a hot serving plate, ready for filling.

Make the mince by browning the meat for a few minutes in the hot fat, then add onion and celery and cook together until onion is transparent. Turn frequently with a fork. Blend in the flour and mustard and cook for a minute, then stir in stock and continue stirring until mixture boils and thickens. Add remainder of ingredients and continue cooking until meat is cooked through, about 20 minutes. Spoon into the baked croustade and serve at once.

A few pieces of red pepper can be kept aside and used to garnish the top of the mince if liked.

## MEAT LOAF

This appetizing mixture is very useful. It can be made into a meat loaf to be baked the night before and served cold with salad next day; it can be baked as individual meat loaves to serve hot as in the following recipe; or it can be made up into patties, dipped in flour, then fried for 5 or 6 minutes on each side and served with potatoes and vegetables. Yet another tasty way is to shape the mixture into small balls about the size of a walnut, thread them on skewers with mushrooms or tomatoes in between and grill as for kebabs (page 109).

I prefer to buy the meat and put it through the mincer with the other ingredients, adding the bread last to absorb the juices left in the mincer. If this is not possible, buy the best quality minced steak from the butcher, and finely chop the vegetables, and crumble the bread.

If mincing the meat yourself, a mixture of beef and pork can be used, or veal and pork for a change.

| | |
|---|---|
| 1 *lb stewing steak* | 2 *thick slices stale bread* |
| ¼ *lb lean pork* | 1 *egg, lightly beaten* |
| 1 *large carrot* | ¼ *teaspoon dry mustard* |
| 1 *medium onion* | 2 *teaspoons Worcestershire sauce* |
| 2 *stalks of celery with leaves* | *salt and pepper to taste* |
| 2 *or* 3 *sprigs of parsley* | 1 *clove of garlic, if liked* |
| *dried or fresh herbs to taste* | |

Put meat, vegetables and herbs through mincer, adding the bread last. Blend well with beaten egg and seasonings, and stand for 30 minutes to blend flavours. Pack mixture into a greased cake tin, or shape into a round and place on a greased ovenproof dish. Bake in a moderate oven (350° F or No 4) for about 1¼ hours, or until cooked through. If browning too much on top, cover with buttered paper or foil.

If loaf was baked in a cake tin, carefully pour off any fat which has accumulated in the tin, then cool loaf. Turn out and wrap in foil or in a plastic bag when quite cold, and store in refrigerator until ready to serve next day. Cut in slices.

These amounts will serve 6.

## MEAT LOAVES WITH SPAGHETTI

These small meat loaves are made with the same mixture as in the preceding recipe, but they are served hot, with spaghetti and a tasty sauce. They require 30 minutes baking time, and the spaghetti cooks for 15 minutes while the loaves are baking.

Form the mixture into 6 small loaf-shapes, and place in a greased baking tin. Bake in a moderate oven (350° F or No 4), and if browning too much on top cover with a piece of buttered paper, or cooking foil. Do not overcook the loaves or they will be dry. When cooked, lift loaves on to a heated ovenproof platter and keep warm while you make the sauce.

Drain off most of the fat in the baking tin, then blend in 2 tablespoons flour as you would for gravy. Add 1½ cups of water and stir until blended and smooth, then add 1 tablespoon tomato paste and 1 beef cube crumbled into ½ cup hot water, and continue stirring until thickened. Season to taste.

Drain the spaghetti well and place round the meat loaves, then pour sauce over the spaghetti. Serve at once.

The meat loaf mixture can be made up the night before, then stored in a covered container in the refrigerator until ready to bake, but do not keep it more than 24 hours before cooking.

## CHEESED BEEFBURGERS

All the preparations for this recipe are done the night before. The beefburgers are wrapped in foil and stored in the refrigerator until ready to cook.

They will need about 12 minutes cooking time.
Serve with fried tomato halves and rice tossed with
chopped parsley.

| | |
|---|---|
| 1 *lb raw minced steak* | ½ *teaspoon dried mixed herbs* |
| 1 *medium-size onion* | *salt and pepper to taste* |
| 1 *oz fat* | *little cooking oil* |
| 2 *oz mushrooms* | 4 *slices processed cheese* |

Peel and chop onion and fry in hot fat until tender. Add
chopped mushrooms and fry a further 3 or 4 minutes. Stir in
the minced steak, herbs and seasonings, mixing well. Allow
mixture to cool slightly, then divide into 8 flat, round cakes.

Wrap these in foil, placing a piece of foil between each
meat cake, and store in refrigerator until ready to cook.

Place unwrapped beefburgers under a pre-heated grill,
using moderate heat, first brushing tops over with a little oil.
Cook for 5 minutes on each side, then top each beefburger
with half a slice of cheese and replace under grill for another
2 minutes, until cheese is bubbling. Serve at once.


## MEAT SCONE-ROUND

This is a change from the usual way of cooking and serving
minced steak, and it makes a hearty meal for a cold night.
The meat can be prepared in the morning before leaving
home, then stored, well covered, in the refrigerator until you
are ready to cook. The scone-round is quickly and easily
made if you have a jar of ready-mix scone dough (see page
170) in the refrigerator, or you can make up the scone-round
in the morning and leave in a cool place ready to put into
the oven at night.

Bake halved, well seasoned tomatoes in the oven at the
same time as the scone-round is cooking, or serve a green
vegetable if preferred.

## SCONE-ROUND

8 oz self-raising flour
1½ oz butter or margarine
½ teaspoon dry mustard

pinch mixed herbs
salt and pepper to taste
milk to mix

### MEAT MIXTURE

1 lb minced steak
1 dessertspoon oil
1 chopped onion
2 tablespoons chopped celery
2 oz mushrooms, chopped

¾ cup hot water
1 tablespoon tomato paste
salt and pepper
1 clove of garlic (optional)

In the morning prepare the scone dough by sieving together the dry ingredients into a basin, then rub in the butter until mixture is like coarse breadcrumbs. Mix to a soft dough with milk, turn on to a lightly floured board and knead lightly, then shape into a round about ¾-inch thick. Place on a greased oven tray and with the back of a knife mark deeply into wedges. Put into a cool place until ready to bake. Brush over with milk and bake in a hot oven (450° F or No 8) for 15 to 20 minutes.

While the scone-round is baking, heat oil in a thick pan and brown the meat, turning with a fork to brown evenly. Add onion, celery and mushrooms and brown for a few minutes. Dissolve tomato paste in hot water and pour over meat mixture, season to taste, and simmer all together for 15 minutes, stirring at intervals. Do not allow to get too dry.

When both scone-round and meat are ready, place scone-round on a heated serving plate, split in halves and spread lightly with butter. Pour meat mixture over bottom half of scone and cover with remaining half. Serve at once, cut in wedges.

If mushrooms are not available, use condensed mushroom soup as the liquid instead of tomato paste and water. Or tomato soup may be substituted instead if desired.

## LAMB AND CORN CASSEROLE

Sweet corn combines well with lamb to make a casserole which re-heats well next day. The casserole is cooked for 1½ hours the night before, then re-heated for 30 minutes before serving.

| | |
|---|---|
| 4 *lamb chump chops* | 2 *carrots, sliced* |
| 1 *dessertspoon fat* | ¾ *pint stock (made with bouillon* |
| 2 *medium onions, sliced* | *cubes)* |
| 1 *cup diced celery* | *salt and pepper* |
| 1 *tablespoon chopped parsley* | 1 *small can of sweet corn* |
| | *flour* |

Trim fat from chops, coat with seasoned flour, and brown on both sides in hot fat. Remove from pan and place in a greased ovenproof casserole. Cook onion and celery in fat remaining in pan, blend in 2 tablespoons flour then stir in stock and bring mixture to the boil, stirring continually. Arrange carrots on top of meat, then add onion and celery mixture, seasoned to taste. Cover and bake in a moderate oven (350° F or No 4) for 1½ hours, or until lamb is tender. Remove from oven and cool, then store in refrigerator until next day.

When ready to re-heat, mix drained corn and chopped parsley together, and place on top of casserole. Cover and cook in a fairly hot oven (400° F or No 6) until bubbling hot. Be sure to remove casserole from 'fridge long enough beforehand to bring it to room temperature, or stand over a basin of hot but not boiling water.

## LAMB AND KIDNEY CASSEROLE

Another useful and tasty casserole, this time with lamb, kidneys and mushrooms as the main ingredients. It needs to be cooked for 1½ hours the night before serving, then re-heated next day, either in the casserole in which it was first cooked, or if you are in a hurry the mixture can be turned into a saucepan to re-heat. In the latter case, the lamb must be watched carefully while it re-heats as it would burn easily.

With so many vegetables in the casserole, it only needs the accompaniment of fluffy mashed potatoes. The amounts serve 6.

| | |
|---|---|
| 2 *lb best end neck of lamb* | 1 *large green pepper, sliced* |
| 3 *or 4 lamb kidneys* | ½ *lb tomatoes, peeled* or 1 *small* |
| 2 *large onions, sliced* | *tin tomatoes* |
| 2 *oz mushrooms, sliced* | 2 *oz fat* |
| 2 *stalks of celery, diced* | 3 *tablespoons flour* |
| *salt and pepper* | 1 *crushed clove of garlic, if liked* |

Wipe the meat and cut into portions. Soak the kidneys in cold water for a few minutes, then skin and core them, and cut into halves. Melt fat in frying pan and fry lamb and kidneys until browned on all sides. Transfer meat to a greased, ovenproof casserole. Brown onions in fat remaining in pan, blend in flour, then stir in 1 pint water or vegetable stock and bring to the boil, stirring continually. Add remainder of ingredients to casserole with meat, then pour onion gravy over the top. Season to taste.

Cover casserole and put into a moderate oven (350° F or No 4) and cook for about 1½ hours, or until meat is tender. Remove from oven and allow to cool, then store overnight in the refrigerator. When ready to re-heat, skim off any fat which may have accumulated on top, and heat in the casserole or in a saucepan on top of the stove.

## RICE AND LAMB PIE

This is an excellent way of using up any left-over lamb from the Sunday joint. The lamb and rice combine to make the crust for a pie, instead of being the filling, then cooked vegetables are added to a white sauce and used as the filling. If the rice and lamb mixture is prepared in the morning before leaving home, the whole dish will only take 30 minutes cooking time.

| | |
|---|---|
| 1 *lb cooked lamb* | 1 *cup white sauce* |
| 1½ *cups cooked rice* | 1½ *cups diced, cooked vegetables* |
| 1 *small onion* | 1 *tablespoon chopped parsley* |
| 1 *egg, beaten* | 3 *tablespoons chopped parsley* |
| *seasonings to taste* | |

Put lamb and onion through the mincer, then mix thoroughly with the rice, egg and seasonings. Press this mixture firmly round the bottom and sides of a well-greased 8-inch pie plate, making an even surface all over. Bake in a very moderate oven (325° F or No 3) for 15 to 20 minutes, or until cooked through and rather crisp, but not too dry.

Combine cooked vegetables with the white sauce, add parsley, and pour into baked lamb case. Sprinkle top with grated cheese and return to oven for a further 10 minutes, or until heated through. Cut in wedges to serve.

If preferred, cooked mushrooms can be added to the sauce instead of vegetables.

## MINTED LAMB CHOPS

If you are rather tired of plain lamb chops, try marinading them in a mixture of mint and lemon juice for new flavour. The chops should be put into the marinade in an earthenware dish before leaving home in the morning, then drained and grilled for dinner. Serve with potato crisps and green peas.

4 *or* 6 *lamb chops*
*salt and pepper*
½ *cup lemon juice*
½ *cup vegetable oil*

1 *clove of garlic, finely chopped*
4 *tablespoons finely chopped mint*
1 *teaspoon grated lemon rind*

Salt and pepper the chops on both sides, and place in a shallow dish just big enough to take them in one layer. Combine all other ingredients and pour over the chops. Put into a cool place (not refrigerator) until you are ready to cook them. If possible, turn the chops over in the marinade before grilling.

They should be grilled for 5 or 6 minutes on each side, and brushed over with the marinade mixture while grilling.

The marinade can be put into a screw-top jar and kept in the refrigerator for at least a week, and used for more chops if desired.

## LAMB CHOPS WITH PINEAPPLE

Another way of adding flavour to lamb chops with a marinade, this time made with pineapple juice. After grilling, the chops are served on slices of pineapple which have been fried in a little butter. If you have a large grill, such as an electric spit-grill, you can cook the chops, pineapple slices and halved tomatoes at the same time.

Put chops into the marinade in the morning, as in previous recipe, and follow the same procedure.

4 *or* 6 *lamb chops*
*salt and pepper*
½ *cup pineapple juice*
¼ *cup oil*

1 *tablespoon grated onion*
1 *crushed clove of garlic*
1 *tablespoon lemon juice*
4 *or* 6 *pineapple slices*

Mix all ingredients except pineapple slices and pour over the chops. Leave until ready to grill, turning once in the marinade. Grill 5 or 6 minutes on each side.

95

# FRICASSEE OF LAMB

Capers give this lamb dish a piquant flavour, and it should be served with a colourful vegetable such as buttered carrots or baked tomatoes. Either chump chops or lamb steaks can be used.

| | |
|---|---|
| 4 *lamb chump chops* | 1 *oz butter or margarine* |
| 1 *medium onion* | 1 *oz plain flour* |
| 1 *medium carrot* | ½ *pint milk* |
| *few sprigs parsley or celery leaves* | *capers* |
| *salt and pepper* | |

Peel and slice onions and carrots and put into a saucepan with parsley or celery leaves. Place chops on top and just cover with cold water. Bring to boil, skim if necessary, then simmer gently for 1 to 1½ hours, or until meat is tender. Remove meat, and when cool, cover and put into refrigerator until next day. Strain stock in saucepan, cool thoroughly and store in refrigerator. Discard vegetables.

When ready to cook place chops in a dish over hot water while you make the sauce. Melt butter or margarine in saucepan, stir in the flour and blend well, then remove from stove and stir in milk and ½ pint of strained stock. Return to heat and stir until boiling and thickened. Add chops and simmer all together for 5 minutes. Season well, then add capers and serve at once.

# LAMB SHANK HOT-POT

The lamb shanks are cooked in a piquant sauce in a saucepan on top of the stove for 1½ hours the night before serving. They are then cooled and stored in the refrigerator. Just before serving, cook for a further 30 minutes, adding the rice.

4 *lamb shanks*
2 *tablespoons fat*
2 *tablespoons flour*
3 *cups boiling water*
1 *tablespoon vinegar*
1 *dessertspoon Worcestershire*
  *sauce*
*salt and pepper*

2 *large onions, chopped*
2 *carrots, sliced*
2 *stalks of celery, chopped with*
  *leaves*
1 *tablespoon chutney*
1 *bay leaf*
2 *tablespoons rice*

Wash and dry the shanks well, then brown in hot fat in a saucepan, turning to brown on all sides. Remove shanks while you fry the onion for a few minutes, then stir in the flour and allow to brown lightly. Stir in water and vinegar, stirring until mixture thickens, then add all other ingredients except rice. Bring to the boil, then cover and simmer gently for 1½ hours, or until shanks are nearly tender. The time depends on the size and age of shanks. Be careful not to overcook. Turn into a basin, allow to cool and store in refrigerator until next day. Remove bay leaf.

When ready to cook next day, turn shanks and vegetable mixture into saucepan and bring to boiling point, adding a little more water if necessary. Add the well-washed rice and boil gently for another 20 to 25 minutes, until rice is tender.

Extra vegetables such as cauliflower or beans can be served with this if desired, and if preferred the rice can be cooked separately and served round the shanks.


## SHEEPS' TONGUES

Next time you see 3 or 4 sheeps' tongues in the butcher's, buy them and prepare them like this. The tongues can be cooked the night before, then re-heated in a savoury sauce, or they are delicious coated with breadcrumbs and fried.

An ox tongue or the smaller calf's tongue can be cooked in the same way, but it will need longer cooking, about 3½ to 4 hours. If you have a pressure cooker it is much quicker and easier. Look for an ox tongue with a smooth skin, which means it comes from a younger animal and should be tender.

Both sheep and ox tongues are good pressed and served cold, and make an ideal dish for a buffet meal, served with salad.

Blanche the tongues before cooking by placing in a saucepan of cold water, bring to the boil, then pour off the water and start again with fresh water. Add a sliced carrot, sliced onion, 1 bay leaf, 6 whole peppercorns, 3 whole cloves, 1 tablespoon lemon juice or vinegar and salt to taste. Bring to the boil, then cover and simmer until tender, about 2½ hours, depending on the age of the lambs.

Remove from saucepan and when cool enough to handle, skin the tongues, and carefully remove gristle and small bones in the root of the tongues. Store covered in refrigerator until ready to cook next day. Strain stock from tongues, cool, and store in 'fridge. Before using next day for sauce, skim fat from top of stock.

## FRIED SHEEPS' TONGUES

| | |
|---|---|
| *3 or 4 tongues* | *3 oz browned breadcrumbs* |
| *1 oz butter, melted* | *fat or oil for frying* |

Cook tongues as above, then cut in halves lengthwise. Dip in melted butter then coat with breadcrumbs on all sides. Fry in hot oil or fat until browned. Be sure tongues are heated through before serving. Serve with any of the following sauces, or as they are with mustard, grilled tomato halves and mashed potatoes.

Ox tongue can be fried in the same way, but it should be cut into slices about ½-inch thick before frying.

# CAPER SAUCE FOR TONGUES

1 *oz butter or margarine*
2 *tablespoons flour*
½ *pint stock from tongues*

½ *teaspoon dry mustard*
1 *teaspoon lemon juice*
1 *tablespoon capers*

Melt butter, then blend in flour and cook for 1 minute. Slowly stir in stock and bring to the boil, stirring all the time. Add remainder of ingredients, then add sliced tongues and simmer gently for several minutes until tongue is heated through. Serve at once. If preferred, the tongues can be put into a casserole, the sauce poured over them, and then re-heated in a moderate oven.

# MUSTARD SAUCE FOR TONGUES

3 *teaspoons cornflour*
1 *teaspoon dry mustard*

1 *teaspoon brown sugar*
½ *pint stock from tongues*

Mix dry ingredients to a smooth paste with a little stock or water. Put stock on to boil, and when it is right on boiling point pour over blended cornflour, stirring well. Return to saucepan and heat until boiling, stirring all the time, then cook for 2 minutes. Serve over sliced tongues which have been re-heated in the tongue stock, then well drained. Or put tongues in a casserole, pour sauce over them and put into a moderate oven until heated through.

## PIQUANT PRUNE SAUCE FOR
## OX TONGUE

1 *oz butter or margarine*
1 *oz flour*
1 *pint tongue stock*
1 *large onion, chopped*

2 *stalks of celery, chopped*
1 *dessertspoon Worcestershire*
*sauce*
1 *tablespoon chutney*
6 *or* 8 *cooked stoned prunes,*
*chopped*

Fry the onion and celery in the butter until tender. Blend in the flour and cook for 1 minute, then stir in stock, stirring until thickened. Add remainder of ingredients and simmer for 2 or 3 minutes. Slice tongue and place in a casserole, pour sauce over the top, cover and re-heat in a moderate oven.

## JELLIED TONGUES

Cook tongues as directed on page 97, using either lamb or ox tongue. Cut lamb tongues in halves lengthwise after removing skin and trimming ends. An ox tongue can be cut in halves lengthwise, or cut in slices then put back into its original shape. If you haven't a meat press, use a cake tin or an earthenware casserole just big enough to take the tongue.

Slices of hard-boiled eggs, slices of pickled cucumber, or shapes cut from canned pimento look nice as a garnish if placed on the bottom of the mould before arranging the tongue on top.

Melt ½ oz gelatine in ½ pint tongue stock, stirring until dissolved, then pour over the tongues, making sure it is distributed through the mould evenly. Cover with a plate and a heavy weight to keep tongue in shape, and leave in a cold place to set. Turn out when ready to serve.

For a whole ox tongue you will need double the above

amount of gelatine mixture. If you have a ring mould, the tongue looks attractive for a party when set in the ring, first garnishing the bottom of the mould as given above. When turned out, the middle of the ring can be filled with cold cooked peas or potato salad, and garnished with lettuce and sliced tomatoes.

## VEAL CUTLETS FARCIE

The amounts given here will serve 6, but if you are only serving 4 you will find the left-over cutlets are very good to serve cold with salad, or they make a tasty addition to a lunch box. All the preparations are done the night before, and the cutlets need to be fried for about 25 minutes before serving.

They are good with noodles boiled for 10 minutes in salted, boiling water, then drained and tossed in melted butter and chopped parsley.

2 *lb pie veal*
1 *cup soft breadcrumbs*
2 *eggs, beaten*
½ *cup warm milk*
4 *oz butter or margarine*

*salt and pepper*
*pinch nutmeg*
1 *cup stock (made with chicken cube)*
½ *cup white wine*

Put the veal twice through the mincer. Mix breadcrumbs and milk together and blend with veal. Add beaten eggs and seasonings, mix well until you have a smooth mixture. Mould into cutlet shapes, place on a flat plate, cover and place in refrigerator until ready to cook.

Melt half the butter or margarine in a thick frying pan and fry half the cutlets at a time, unless you have a pan big enough to take them all at once. Turn to cook on both sides for about 10 minutes each side, until golden brown and crisp. Keep hot while you fry remainder in same way, using rest of butter. When all the cutlets are cooked and taken from the pan, add stock and wine, stirring well, then boil quickly to reduce. Strain and serve some over the cutlets, which should be placed in a ring of noodles. Serve remainder of gravy separately.

Pork can be used instead of veal if preferred.

## VEAL PAPRIKA

After preparing, this dish is cooked in a casserole for 45 to 50 minutes, then cooled and refrigerated until next day. When ready to cook it is re-heated in the oven for 15 minutes then sour cream is added and it is cooked for another 5 minutes.

Rice is cooked while casserole is re-heating, and served as a border round the veal. Piquant Tomatoes (page 115) would go well as a vegetable with the blandness of the veal.

| | |
|---|---|
| 2 *lb pie veal* | 1 *cup finely chopped onion* |
| 1 *oz flour* | 1 *cup stock or white wine* |
| 1 *teaspoon paprika* | 1 *cup sour cream* |
| *salt and pepper to taste* | ½ *to* ¾ *lb rice* |
| 2 *oz butter or lard* | |

Cut veal into 1-inch pieces. Mix flour, paprika, salt and pepper in a clean paper bag and toss veal in the dry mixture until well coated. Heat fat in a thick pan and brown veal on all sides, then lift with a slotted spoon and place in a greased casserole. Cook onion in fat remaining in pan until golden, stirring to prevent burning, then add remaining flour mixture and blend in with onions. Stir in stock or wine, cook for a few minutes and pour over veal in casserole. Cover and cook in moderate oven (350° F or No 4) for 45 to 50 minutes, until veal is tender. Leave in casserole until cool, then store in refrigerator.

Remove casserole from refrigerator 15 minutes before

re-heating. If more gravy is needed, add a little more stock or wine, stirring well, but remember that the cream must be added as well. If preferred, yoghurt can be substituted for the sour cream, but be careful it does not boil when re-heating.

Chopped parsley can be tossed into the rice for extra colour contrast.

## VEAL CHOPS IN FOIL

Only the sauce is prepared the night before for this delicious recipe, which will take 30 to 35 minutes cooking time before serving.

Baked tomatoes (page 113) and French fried potatoes would be good with this, or tender young peas.

4 *medium-size veal chops*
6 *tablespoons butter or margarine*
1 *clove of garlic (if liked)*
2 *tablespoons chopped shallots or onion*
½ *lb mushrooms, chopped*
1 *tablespoon lemon juice*

¼ *pint chicken stock*
2 *tablespoons tomato purée*
2 *tablespoons soft breadcrumbs*
2 *tablespoons chopped parsley*
4 *thin slices cooked ham*
*salt and pepper to taste*
4 *pieces of cooking foil*

Melt 3 tablespoons butter in a pan and fry garlic for a minute, then remove. Cook the shallots and mushrooms in the butter for a few minutes, then add lemon juice and continue cooking until mushrooms are cooked, about 5 minutes. Add chicken stock, tomato purée, breadcrumbs and chopped parsley, seasoning to taste, and cook together until you have a soft paste, without letting it become too dry. Store in refrigerator, covered, until next day.

Cut the foil into 4 oval shapes large enough to enclose each chop completely, with plenty of turn-over for sealing.

When ready to cook, melt remaining butter in pan large enough to take the four chops in one layer, and sauté them gently until golden on both sides (5 to 6 minutes). While chops are browning, heat the mushroom mixture over boiling water.

Brush the foil ovals with a little cooking oil, place a ham slice on one half of each oval and coat with the mushroom mixture. Place a veal chop on this and cover with more of the mushroom sauce. Fold the foil over and crimp the edges firmly together to seal.

Place the foil parcels on a baking sheet and bake in a moderately hot oven (400° F or No 6) for 25 to 30 minutes, by which time the chops should have been cooked through and be tender.

Serve each parcel on a heated plate, opening the foil slightly to let the very good aroma escape and give an idea of the good food within.


# SAUSAGE COBBLER WITH MUSTARD SAUCE

Preparations for this dish are done in the morning before leaving home, and are not very arduous. The sausages are fried with the onions, then placed in an ovenproof casserole, ready for the next stage of the cooking. The topping batter can be mixed in the morning if time permits, but it only takes a few minutes to prepare before cooking. The white sauce can be made the night before and stored in the 'fridge until needed (page 141).

1 *lb pork sausages*
1 *rasher fat bacon*
2 *onions, sliced thin*
4 *oz self-raising flour*

*salt and pepper*
1 *egg*
1 *cup milk*

FOR THE SAUCE
½ *pint fairly thin white sauce*
2 *teaspoons mixed mustard*
1 *tablespoon chopped mixed pickles*

1 *tablespoon vinegar*
1 *teaspoon chopped parsley*

In the morning fry the bacon in a hot pan until fairly crisp on both sides. Remove and cut into dice. In fat in pan fry the sausages and the onions, turning to brown evenly. Remove sausages from pan and drain off any surplus fat, then cut into 1-inch pieces. Place in greased ovenproof casserole with the bacon and onions, and cover when cool to prevent drying out.

To make the cobbler sift flour, salt and pepper into a bowl, make a well in the centre and add unbeaten egg. Fold flour in from sides, gradually adding milk to make a smooth batter. If necessary, this batter will not suffer from standing all day, until ready to use at night. Pour over the sausage and onion mixture, and bake in a hot oven (425° F or No 7) for 30 minutes, or until topping is well risen and golden on top. Cut in wedges to serve with mustard sauce.

Make the sauce while the cobbler is baking. Fold mustard and pickles into sauce, then gradually add the vinegar. Re-heat over hot water, but do not allow sauce to boil. Add parsley just before serving.

## SAUSAGE AND POTATO ROLLS

All the preparations for these rolls are done the night before, ready to be cooked for 20 to 25 minutes in a hot oven before serving.

Baked tomatoes (page 113) and a green vegetable would be a good accompaniment.

| | |
|---|---|
| 1 *lb sinless sausages* (8) | *butter or margarine* |
| *little fat* | 1 *egg yolk* |
| 2 *lb potatoes* | 1 *dessertspoon milk* |
| *salt and pepper to taste* | *flour* |
| *chopped parsley* | 1 *beef cube* |

Heat a little fat in a thick frying pan and fry sausage all over

D*

until lightly browned. Remove from pan and drain well on absorbent paper. Drain off fat from pan, add 1 cup of water and bring to boil, loosening the crust on bottom of pan. Strain and keep in refrigerator, covered, until next day.

While sausages are cooking, boil peeled potatoes until soft, drain and mash well with a little milk and butter until smooth and creamy, seasoning to taste, then add chopped parsley. Spread potatoes out on board and press into a rectangle about ¼-inch thick, then cut into 8 pieces. Cover each sausage with potatoes, pressing into rolls. Place in refrigerator until 15 minutes before cooking time.

When ready to cook, brush the rolls over with a little beaten egg yolk and place in a single layer in a greased baking dish. Bake in a hot oven (400° F or No 6) for 20 to 25 minutes, turning to brown evenly.

While sausage rolls are cooking, prepare the gravy by thickening with a little flour and adding the beef cube, stirring until smooth and free of lumps.

The tomatoes can bake in the oven at the same time as the rolls.


## PORK CHOPS AND CAPER CASSEROLE

After preparing, this casserole is cooked for 30 minutes in a moderately hot oven, then cooled and stored in refrigerator until its final heating. Remove from refrigerator at least 20 minutes before putting into the oven, and cook for 15 to 20 minutes before serving.

Quick shredded cabbage (page 121) and oven-browned potatoes (page 125) would be good served with this casserole.

| | |
|---|---|
| 4 *pork chops* | ¼ *pint stock or water* |
| 2 *tablespoons cooking oil* | 1 *tablespoon capers* |
| 2 *oz flour* | *salt and pepper to taste* |
| 15 *oz can tomato juice* | 1 *clove of garlic, if liked* |

Trim chops of excess fat. Heat oil in frying pan, and fry chops for 2 to 3 minutes on each side. Drain well and place in a greased casserole. Blend flour to oil in pan, then stir in tomato juice and stock, stirring until it thickens slightly. Add crushed clove of garlic (if using) and capers, with salt and pepper to taste. Pour over chops in casserole, cover and cook in moderately hot oven (375° F or No 5) for 30 minutes.

Cool casserole and store in refrigerator until needed.

Cook in moderately hot oven for 15 to 20 minutes, until heated through and bubbling, but test chops for tenderness, as some are thicker than others and take more time.

## FRUITED PORK CHOPS

If you like the combination of pork with fruit, you will enjoy this casserole, which can be cooked the night before, then just re-heated before serving.

*4 pork chops*
*salt, pepper and dry mustard*
*2 tablespoons pork or bacon fat*
*1 large onion, sliced*
*1 tablespoon cornflour*

*4 slices pineapple*
*4 prunes*
*1 cup pineapple syrup*
*1 tablespoon lemon juice or vinegar*

Soak prunes in hot water for half an hour if they are not already tenderized. If preferred, seeded raisins may be used instead of prunes, using about 1 dozen, and plumping them in hot water for a few minutes before using.

Mix salt, pepper and dry mustard together and rub over the chops on both sides. Heat the fat and brown chops, turning to brown each side, then transfer to a greased casserole. Fry the onion in fat remaining in pan until golden brown, then arrange round the chops in casserole. Place a pineapple

slice on each chop, add a prune in the centre of each, or
scatter with raisins. Heat the pineapple syrup in the pan
in which chops were browned, then stir in the cornflour
blended with a little water, stirring until clear and thick. Add
lemon juice, and more water if necessary, then pour over
casserole. Cover and cook in moderate oven (350° F or
No 4), for about 1 hour, or until chops are tender. Cool and
store in refrigerator until next day. Re-heat until bubbling.

## PORK GALANTINE

During the summer it is useful occasionally to be able to
prepare a tasty galantine or meat loaf which can be served
cold with salad the next day. This recipe makes a nice change
from cold meat, and it is simple to prepare, needing to be
steamed for 1½ hours the day before serving.

| | |
|---|---|
| 1 *lb pork sausage meat* | *pinch dried mixed herbs* |
| 2 *oz lean streaky bacon* | 1 *teaspoon Worcestershire sauce* |
| 1 *egg, beaten slightly* | 1 *teaspoon dry mustard* |
| 4 *tablespoons dried breadcrumbs* | *salt and pepper* |
| 2 *tablespoons chopped parsley* | 1 *beef extract cube* |
| | ¼ *pint hot water* |

Remove bacon rinds and chop bacon very small. Dissolve
beef cube in hot water. Mix chopped bacon, sausage meat,
breadcrumbs, egg and seasonings together in a bowl, blending well together, then add liquid ingredients to make a
fairly soft mixture.

Grease a 1-pint basin and fill with prepared mixture.
Cover with aluminium foil and steam in a saucepan of
steadily boiling water for 1½ hours. Be sure to keep boiling
water replenished as it boils away in saucepan.

When cooked, allow galantine to cool completely, then

store in refrigerator until next day. Turn out and cut in slices or wedges to serve, accompanied by a salad. Sliced hard-boiled eggs and sliced tomatoes can be arranged round the galantine as a garnish.

## SHISH KEBABS

If you have one of those very useful spit-roasters, either electric or gas, you probably know how useful kebabs can be as a cook-at-the-last-minute meal. All kinds of food can be threaded on skewers and grilled, and the spit-roaster has the advantage of turning the skewers automatically, thus cooking the food evenly. But even if you cook your kebabs in the oven or under the grill of your stove, you can make up some very tasty combinations of meat, fish or chicken and vegetables.

Care should be taken to ensure that all foods are cooked at the same time, and it is usually necessary to have a sauce for basting, not only to keep the food from drying out, but also to add flavour. Ingredients used for kebabs are frequently marinaded before cooking, and this can be done in the morning before leaving home, although steak or lamb can be left in the marinade overnight if more convenient.

If you have an outdoor barbecue, these kebabs are excellent when cooked over glowing charcoal, turning frequently to cook evenly.

Long steel skewers are a necessity for all kinds of kebabs, although the Japanese do use bamboo skewers for their delicious teriyaki, just as the Javanese do for sate. The usual accompaniment to kebabs is rice.

# TURKISH KEBABS

The lamb in this recipe should be marinaded for at least 12 hours before cooking, and will not suffer if left for 24, so prepare it the night before you want to serve. It can be covered and left in refrigerator, but remove half an hour before cooking.

| | |
|---|---|
| 2 *lb lamb, cut from the leg 1-inch thick* | 8 *small onions, par-boiled* |
| | 4 *small, firm tomatoes* |
| 2 *small green peppers* | 8 *mushroom caps* |

FOR THE MARINADE
| | |
|---|---|
| 6 *tablespoons olive oil* | |
| 4 *tablespoons dry sherry or lemon juice* | 1 *small onion, chopped* |
| | 2 *tablespoons chopped parsley* |
| 1 *clove of garlic, chopped* | *salt and freshly ground pepper* |

Combine all ingredients for the marinade and mix well. Cut lamb into pieces ½-inch thick and add to marinade, mixing well, and making sure all the meat pieces are covered. Cover and leave in 'fridge until ready to cook. If possible, turn the meat several times in the marinade.

When ready to cook, drain the meat and place on long skewers with other ingredients alternating with the meat cubes. There should be four pieces of meat on each skewer. Brush the filled skewers over with marinade mixture and grill, turning frequently and brushing over with marinade several times. Serve on a bed of fluffy cooked rice.

# RUSSIAN SHASHLIK

In Russia they also use lamb for their skewer cooking, and alternate marinaded cubes of lamb with small button mushrooms.

MARINADE

| | |
|---|---|
| ¼ *cup olive oil* | *salt and freshly ground pepper* |
| 3 *tablespoons lemon juice* | 2 *medium onions, chopped* |

Cut lamb into cubes and soak in marinade overnight. When ready to cook, dip mushrooms in the marinade and thread on long skewers alternately with the lamb cubes. Baste with the marinade several times while grilling. Serve on a mound of boiled rice which has been tossed with chopped parsley or chives.

## LAMB AND PINEAPPLE KEBABS

Alternate cubes of lamb, pineapple and bacon are delicious on skewers, and for a change are served with buttered noodles.

MARINADE

| | |
|---|---|
| ¼ *cup salad oil* | 1 *crushed clove of garlic* |
| ¼ *cup pineapple juice* | 1 *tablespoon chopped parsley* |
| *salt and pepper* | 1 *teaspoon soya sauce* |

Leave the lamb cubes in the marinade for about 12 hours. Thread on skewers alternately with the pineapple cubes, placing a square of fatty bacon between each one. Baste with pineapple marinade while grilling.

## STEAK ON SKEWERS

Good quality steak is needed for these kebabs, as they are grilled fairly quickly, but the marinade helps to tenderize the meat, which should be cut about 1-inch thick. Alternate the steak cubes with small par-boiled onions, squares of sweet red pepper and mushrooms. Small squares of bacon can be threaded between the ingredients if liked.

MARINADE
¼ *cup salad oil*
¼ *cup dry sherry or vinegar*
2 *teaspoons Worcestershire sauce*
1 *teaspoon lemon juice*

1 *clove of garlic, crushed*
*salt and freshly ground pepper*
1 *tablespoon chopped onion*
2 *sprigs parsley*

Soak steak in the above marinade overnight. Brush over skewers when filled and use to baste kebabs as they grill.

## SUMMER KEBABS

These kebabs are marinaded in the usual way, but they are not cooked before serving, but served with a salad as a cold meal.

8 *oz cold, cooked meat*
8 *small, firm tomatoes*
4 *pineapple rings*

4 *pickled onions*
½ *a cucumber*

MARINADE
2 *tablespoons salad oil*
2 *tablespoons vinegar*
1 *tablespoon pineapple juice*

*pinch each of salt, pepper, mus-*
*tard and sugar*
1 *teaspoon chopped parsley*

Cut meat into squares (ham is excellent for this); halve tomatoes, peel cucumber and cut into squares, also pineapple. Leave in marinade for 30 minutes, then put on skewers and serve.

# Vegetables

There are a lot of good-quality frozen and canned vegetables available today, but many housewives prefer to use fresh ones when they are available during the summer, and use the frozen and canned ones during the winter when the gardens are bare. Of course it is always wise to keep a few cans of vegetables in the cupboard for an emergency, winter or summer.

Most vegetables can be prepared overnight and stored in plastic bags in the refrigerator ready for cooking, without any loss of flavour, but few fresh vegetables are as good when cooked and re-heated later on. The only exceptions to this is when using left-over cooked vegetables as a stuffing for tomatoes as given on page 115, or on the rare occasions when you want to have a good 'fry-up' with cooked potatoes and vegetables chopped and fried together to form a cake, browned on both sides in a little cooking oil.

Cooked vegetables are also most useful for salads, and it is a good idea to cook extra amounts of such vegetables as peas, beans, carrots, and potatoes to use in salad meals.

Cooked potatoes can be used in a number of ways to serve next day, several suggestions being given in the following pages.

## BAKED TOMATOES

Tomatoes are one of the most useful vegetables (or are they fruits?) available to the busy housewife, as they can be served in so many ways, either hot or cold.

Whichever way you are serving tomatoes, they will be

improved by the addition of salt, pepper, a very little sugar, and a touch of garlic (optional, but recommended).

If you are using the oven for dinner, bake tomatoes at the same time – or good results can be obtained by grilling, but here care should be taken not to brown them too much.

For baking, cut firm, ripe tomatoes in halves, brush the cut sides over with a little cooking oil, sprinkle with salt, pepper and sugar, and place on a baking sheet. Bake in a moderate oven until soft, but do not over-cook or they will split. Cook under the griller in the same way.

A sprinkle of mixed herbs adds extra flavour, or if serving with lamb, add a sprinkle of finely chopped mint.

Green tomatoes can be cooked in the same way, but add a little extra sugar and cook for a longer period.

## CREAMED TOMATOES

The only preparations needed beforehand for these is to peel the tomatoes, choosing large, firm ones, not too ripe (they will peel easily if you immerse them in boiling water for a few seconds first). Actual cooking time takes 12 to 15 minutes.

| | |
|---|---|
| *2 or 3 large tomatoes* | *butter or margarine* |
| *plain flour* | *brown sugar* |
| *salt and pepper* | *2 tablespoons cream* |
| *½ teaspoon curry powder* | |

Cut the tomatoes into slices about ½-inch thick. Mix salt, pepper and curry powder with the flour and coat the tomato slices on both sides with the seasoned flour. Melt butter or margarine in a large frying pan and when hot but not browned, add tomato slices, cooking as many slices as possible in one layer. Cook until lightly browned, then turn the slices carefully with a spatula and sprinkle lightly with brown sugar. When other sides are browned, turn them again and sprinkle with a little more sugar. Cook until tender, but firm and unbroken, and remove from pan to a heated serving dish. Stir the cream into the pan and stir with the residue in the bottom, blending as smooth as possible, then pour over tomato slices and serve at once.

Good with grilled fish or veal chops.


## BAKED TOMATOES PIQUANT

These can be cooked under the griller if more convenient, but preferably they should be cooked in the oven if it is in use. The tomatoes can be prepared in the morning before leaving home, but they only take a few minutes, and could be left until just before they are to be cooked. Cooking time is 10 to 12 minutes.

| | |
|---|---|
| 4 *large firm tomatoes* | ½ *teaspoon Worcestershire sauce* |
| 1 *tablespoon finely chopped onion* | *pinch sugar* |
| 1 *teaspoon dry mustard* | *salt and pepper* |
| | 1 *tablespoon butter* |

Cut each tomato in half, and cut an X in the middle of each cut half. Combine onion, mustard, sauce, sugar, salt and pepper and spread over cut side of each tomato half, pressing down into cuts. Place a small pat of butter on top of each one, and place in shallow ovenproof dish which has been rubbed round with butter. Bake in fairly hot oven for 10 to 12 minutes, until heated through and bubbling on top.

Excellent with a grill.


## TOMATOES WITH VEGETABLE FILLINGS

Cold cooked vegetables can be combined with a little white

sauce (page 141) and used to fill hollowed out tomatoes. These are then placed in a buttered ovenproof dish and baked for 20 to 25 minutes, depending on size. Sprinkle tops with breadcrumbs and dot with butter, or with grated cheese if suitable to the dish being served.

Or the cooked vegetables can be combined with cold, cooked rice, and a little mayonnaise added to bind together. Season the hollowed out tomatoes well, fill and bake as above. Do not serve potatoes with rice-filled tomatoes.

Canned sweet corn, combined with chopped green peppers or cooked peas makes another good filling for tomatoes. The pulp scooped out of the tomatoes can be chopped and added to the sweet corn, with salt and pepper and a pat of butter, then bake as above.

## STUFFED GREEN PEPPERS

These can be served as a vegetable course to accompany a grill or plain grilled fish, or they could make a luncheon dish, served either hot or cold.

The cheese and carrots can be grated the night before and stored in plastic bags in refrigerator, along with the cooked rice. The peppers can also be prepared overnight if preferred, but do not fill them until just before cooking. They will take about 15 to 20 minutes baking time.

| | |
|---|---|
| 4 *large, evenly sized green peppers* | *salt and pepper* |
| 1 *cup grated cheese* | 2 *teaspoons scraped onion* |
| 1 *cup cooked rice* | 1 *tablespoon butter or margarine* |
| 2 *raw, grated carrots* | *paprika* |

Choose peppers as nearly the same size as possible, with good shapes. Cut a slice from the stem end and carefully scoop out the seeds and inside pith. Wash inside and out, then par-boil for a few minutes. Drain well and when quite cold store in refrigerator.

When ready to cook, mix together rice, carrot, cheese, scraped onion, salt and pepper and fill the peppers. Dot each one with butter, sprinkle lightly with paprika, and place in a buttered ovenproof dish, making sure they are standing firmly upright. Bake for 15 to 20 minutes until cooked through and tops are golden brown.

## BEETROOT AND ONION BAKE

This unusual and very tasty mixture can be served either hot as a vegetable or cold with a salad. It can be cooked the night before, then cooled and stored in the casserole in which it was cooked, ready to be re-heated the following night.

| | |
|---|---|
| 1 *lb young beetroot* | 2 *tablespoons sugar* |
| 2 *medium onions* | 4 *or 5 whole cloves* |
| ½ *cup orange juice* | 1 *bay leaf* |
| 2 *tablespoons lemon juice* | *salt and pepper* |

Peel and slice the beets thinly, and peel and slice the onions as thinly as possible. Put beet and onions in alternate layers in a casserole. Combine remainder of ingredients and pour over layers. Cover and bake in a moderately hot oven (375° F or No 5) for 1 to 1¼ hours, until beet is tender.

If serving hot as a vegetable, pour off the juices in the casserole and thicken with a little cornflour, adding a teaspoon of butter. Heat beet and onions in the sauce and serve at once.

## CELERY HEARTS

If serving as a vegetable, these are best cooked immediately before serving, but if to be served cold as an hors d'oeuvre or with a salad, they should be cooked the night before and stored in the refrigerator.

| | |
|---|---|
| 2 *heads of celery* | 1 *small onion* |
| 2 *cups chicken stock (made with* | *dash of pepper* |
| *cube if necessary)* | 2 *teaspoons cornflour* |

Use only the celery hearts (the remainder can be used in soup or a casserole). Leave only about 2 inches above the heart, then cut each heart lengthwise into four. Wash well without separating the stalks. Cook in boiling soup stock with the onion until tender, about 15 minutes, then drain well and keep hot while you thicken the stock with cornflour blended with a little water. Season with pepper and pour over celery. Serve at once.

If to be served cold, drain well, then cover with French dressing (page 148), turning occasionally in the dressing while cooling. Store covered in refrigerator overnight, then serve on a bed of watercress and garnish with thin strips of anchovy and pimento.

## PARSNIP FRITTERS

These are prepared the night before, ready to be fried just before serving. Carrots can be prepared in the same way, or use a mixture of mashed potatoes and carrots combined.

| | |
|---|---|
| 4 *good-sized young parsnips* | *salt and pepper* |
| 1 *tablespoon plain flour* | *fat or cooking oil* |
| 1 *egg* | |

Scrape or thinly peel the parsnips, slice and put into cold, salted water, then bring to boil. Cook until tender, then drain well and mash until smooth, or put through an electric blender. Add flour and beaten egg, and correct seasoning. Mix well, then shape mixture into patties. Wrap in polythene and store in refrigerator until ready to cook.

Heat fat or oil in frying pan and fry fritters until golden brown on both sides. Drain on absorbent paper and serve at once.

The fritters can be dipped in browned breadcrumbs before frying if liked.

## BELGIAN CHICORY

This is best cooked immediately before serving, as the chicory is inclined to discolour if left after cooking. It will take 25 minutes to cook, and another 3 or 4 minutes to cook the sauce.

| | |
|---|---|
| 1 *lb chicory* | ½ *oz cornflour* |
| 2 *teaspoons lemon juice* | *salt and pepper* |
| *milk* | 2 *oz grated cheese* |
| 1 *oz butter or margarine* | |

Wash and trim the chicory, and put into a saucepan of boiling, salted water, adding the lemon juice. Boil gently for 25 minutes, until tender. Drain well, saving the liquid in which chicory was cooked, and making up to ½ pint with milk. Melt butter in a small pan and blend in cornflour, then gradually blend in liquid, stirring until it thickens and boils. Boil gently for 3 minutes, then add half the cheese, and stir until well blended with sauce. Serve sauce over the chicory, sprinkling with remainder of cheese just before serving.

If time permits, the chicory can be put into a heatproof dish, covered with the sauce, sprinkled with cheese and browned under a hot griller.

# LEEKS AU GRATIN

The leeks can be prepared and cooked the night before, covered with the sauce, then re-heated for 15 to 20 minutes before serving.

Before cooking, the leeks should be very well washed, as they are a very gritty vegetable. Trim the roots and cut off the tops, but leave about 2 inches of the green part if the leeks are young. Split leeks lengthwise to within 1 inch of the root, then wash them thoroughly under running water.

If you prefer to serve leeks cooked quite plainly, simmer them in boiling, salted water for 20 minutes, then drain well. Sprinkle with finely chopped parsley and add a little melted butter. Serve at once.

| | |
|---|---|
| 8 *medium-size leeks* | 1 *teaspoon made mustard* |
| 3 *tablespoons butter or margarine* | 1 *teaspoon lemon juice* |
| 3 *tablespoons flour* | *salt and pepper to taste* |
| ¾ *pint hot milk* | *fresh breadcrumbs* |
| 4 *oz grated Gruyère cheese* | 2 *teaspoons butter* |

Cook leeks as directed above, then drain well and place in a buttered ovenproof dish.

Make the sauce by melting the butter or margarine and blending in the flour until smooth. Allow to cook for a few minutes, remove from heat and slowly stir in a little of the hot milk, stirring until blended. Add remainder of milk and cook, stirring constantly, until mixture boils. Add half the quantity of grated cheese and continue stirring until it has melted into sauce. Add mustard, lemon juice, salt and pepper, and cook for 1 minute, then pour over the leeks. Allow to cool, then cover and store in refrigerator until next day.

Remove from refrigerator 15 minutes before cooking time, mix crumbs with remainder of grated cheese and sprinkle over the sauce, dot with butter and put into a moderately hot oven (375° F or No 5) for about 20 minutes, until mixture bubbles and top is golden brown. Serve at once.

## ASPARAGUS

Asparagus is usually served as a separate course rather than as an accompaniment to a main dish. But either freshly cooked or canned asparagus tips make a delicious garnish to hot or cold chicken or veal dishes.

If you want to serve it hot before the main course, prepare the asparagus in the morning, and cook for 10 to 15 minutes just before serving. Serve at once with hot melted butter and a dusting of paprika. Or cook the night before, allow to get cold, and store in a covered dish in refrigerator until just before serving time. It can be served with French dressing or mayonnaise as you prefer.

It can also be served au gratin, as in the recipe for leeks (page 120).

To cook, choose a deep saucepan in which the stalks can stand upright with only their tips out of water. Wash the asparagus well as they grow in sandy soil which clings. It is easier to handle the stalks if you tie them together before putting into saucepan of boiling water, to which a little salt has been added. Cover and simmer for 10 to 15 minutes, depending on the thickness of the stalks, until just tender. Do not overcook or they will be mushy and break up. Drain well and serve as desired.

## QUICK SHREDDED CABBAGE

The cabbage can be prepared in the morning before leaving home, and may be shredded ready to cook if stored in a plastic bag in the refrigerator – but be sure it is tightly sealed.

Cut cabbage into quarters and cut away the thick core and ribs. Wash well, adding a little salt to the water, then drain and shred finely. Peel and chop a small onion and a clove of garlic if liked.

Melt some butter or margarine in a large saucepan and cook the onion and garlic until soft but not browned. Add shredded cabbage, season with salt and pepper and 1 teaspoon of lemon juice or vinegar and cook, tightly covered, for 8 to 10 minutes, shaking the pan at intervals. Serve at once.

Some chopped green pepper can be added to the cabbage if liked, or follow the German example and add a sprinkle of caraway seeds as the cabbage cooks.

## HERBED CARROTS

These are delicious to serve with chicken or fish, and add colour to a plain dish. They should be cooked just before serving.

| | |
|---|---|
| 1 *lb young carrots* | 1 *tablespoon each of finely* |
| *salt and pepper* | *chopped parsley and chives* |
| 2 *oz butter* | *few sprigs fresh thyme, chopped* |

Cut the carrots into strips about the thickness of a pencil, and all the same length. Cook in boiling, salted water until tender, about 10 minutes, but they should still be a little crisp so do not overcook. Drain well and add butter to the pan with the chopped herbs, and continue cooking for 2 or 3 minutes more, tossing the carrots occasionally in the herb butter. Sprinkle with pepper and serve at once.

Young celery, cut in pieces the same size as the carrots, can be added to the carrots to cook together if liked for a change.

## CARROT AND RICE CAKES

These can be made up the night before, ready to cook next day. They make a good breakfast dish, topped with a grilled half tomato, or can be served as a vegetable with a plain grill.

1 *lb young carrots*
6 *oz cooked rice*
2 *eggs*
*salt and pepper*
½ *teaspoon sugar*

*pinch ground nutmeg*
*browned breadcrumbs*
2 *oz butter or margarine*
*flour*

Cook the carrots until tender, then put through food mill or electric blender. Cook rice and drain well, then rinse under cold water and drain again. Mix rice, carrots, seasonings and 1 beaten egg together, and form into flat cakes. Wrap in foil and store in refrigerator until ready to cook.

Dip the carrot cakes into flour, then into the remaining egg lightly beaten, then into breadcrumbs, until well coated all over. Fry cakes in butter, turning to brown both sides. Serve as desired.

## SWEET CORN FRITTERS

An excellent accompaniment to fried chicken or with veal chops, these are made with canned sweet corn just before serving.

10 *or* 11 *oz can of sweet corn*
1 *large egg*
2 *oz flour*

*salt and pepper*
*cooking oil*

Drain the corn well. Lightly beat the egg into the flour, season with salt and pepper and mix in corn. Heat a little oil in a thick frying pan and drop spoonfuls of the corn mixture into the pan, frying until golden on both sides.

These are also delicious served for supper, topped with thick slices of fried tomato and sprinkled with chopped parsley.

## POTATOES

Potatoes can be cooked overnight, and warmed up in various ways for dinner next day; but if you want them mashed, cook them fresh just before serving and mash them at once. Nothing tastes more like blotting paper than warmed-up mashed potatoes – but you can cook double quantities and make potato cakes for the next night.

*Potato Cakes :* Mash the potatoes in the usual way with butter, milk, salt and pepper, but also beat in a small egg and some finely chopped parsley or chives. Let the mixture get cold, then shape into patties. When ready to cook, dip each cake into lightly beaten egg, then into browned breadcrumbs and fry on both sides in hot fat until golden brown.

*Potato and Vegetable Patties :* Make up the mashed potato mixture as directed above, but add any left-over cooked vegetables such as finely chopped green beans, carrots, or onions to the potato and egg before forming into patties, then fry as above.

*Duchesse Potatoes :* Prepare creamy mashed potatoes as above. Put mixture into a forcing bag with a $\frac{1}{2}$-inch rose nozzle and pipe potato in whirls on to a greased baking sheet. Lightly brush over with beaten egg and bake in a moderately hot oven (375° F or No 5) for 15 to 20 minutes until golden brown.

*Golden Potato Balls :* Another variation of the first recipe is to form the potato mixture into small balls with floured hands. Leave in a cool place until ready to cook. Coat first in beaten egg, then in browned crumbs, and fry in deep hot fat for about 5 minutes until golden brown all over.

*Oven-browned Potatoes:* Choose fairly large, evenly sized potatoes and scrub well. Put into boiling, salted water and cook for 30 minutes, or until tender, but still firm. Cool and put aside until tomorrow. When ready to cook, cut each potato in halves, cut an X in the cut side, and brush all over with cooking oil. Stand on the rack in a hot oven and bake for 20 to 25 minutes, until heated through and lightly browned all over. Press to open X, and insert a tiny pat of butter. Sprinkle with salt and pepper and serve at once.

## POTATOES CHARLOTTE

Serve this delicious potato dish with a grill, and when tomatoes are in season, bake halved tomatoes in the oven at the same time as the potatoes.

The potatoes can be cooked the night before and left whole, then the dish can be prepared just before cooking. It requires 25 to 30 minutes baking time in a moderate oven.

| | |
|---|---|
| 3 *or* 4 *good-sized boiled potatoes* | 3 *oz grated cheese* |
| 1 *medium onion, chopped small* | ½ *cup hot milk* |
| 1 *tablespoon butter or margarine* | *paprika or finely chopped parsley* |

Cut potatoes into ¼-inch slices. Cook the chopped onion in the butter until soft but not browned. Put a layer of potato slices in a greased ovenproof casserole, sprinkle with one-third of the grated cheese, and some of the onion. Add a little paprika or chopped parsley. Repeat these layers until potatoes are used up, finishing with a layer of grated cheese. Heat the milk in the same pan as the onion was cooked in and pour over the potatoes. Bake in a moderate oven (350° F or No 4) until mixture bubbles and cheese is melted and golden on top. If cheese browns too quickly, cover with a piece of buttered paper.

# Salads

Salads come into two categories – those which form the main dish for a meal, usually during the summer, or those which are served as a separate course for dinner or to accompany the main course.

You will find both kinds here, which you can use to suit your own personal requirements and tastes. Except in two or three cases, the ingredients for the salads are prepared either overnight or in the morning before leaving home, and then assembled just before serving.

This keeps all ingredients fresh and crisp, and with a better appearance, which is very important with salads. Nothing looks more unappetizing than limp lettuce and dried-up vegetables masquerading as salad, and the little extra time taken in assembling the ingredients with an eye for colour and appearance is well worthwhile.

A simple salad can be given extra flavour by serving with a piquant dressing. A number of these will be found on pages 146–48, in the chapter on Sauces and Dressings.

You have a choice of greens to use for salads, with plain cabbage lettuce, Cos or Density lettuce, chicory or endive, watercress and young cabbage. With the exception of chicory, they should all be washed and well dried, then stored in the plastic box in the bottom of your refrigerator or in plastic bags. Salad greens should never be put into the freezing compartment.

Peppers can be washed, seeded and sliced beforehand, and stored in plastic box or bag; carrots should be scrubbed or thinly peeled and sliced or grated as needed, then stored in refrigerator in a plastic bag, and tomatoes washed, peeled and stored in refrigerator box – but keep them away from the freezing compartment.

Extra green vegetables such as peas, French beans or broad beans can be cooked the night before with the dinner vegetables and stored in the refrigerator to include in a salad next day; and the same with potatoes, which can be used for a potato salad. Rice is another ingredient which can be cooked in extra quantities, then used for a salad next day.

## AVOCADO AND CREAM CHEESE SALAD

Avocados make a delicious salad meal, or they can be served as the first course for dinner. The filling can be prepared in the morning before leaving home, then the salad can be put together just before serving, taking no more than 10 minutes to finish.

| | |
|---|---|
| 2 *large or* 4 *small ripe avocados* | *salt and pepper to taste* |
| 1 *tablespoon lemon juice* | 1 *tablespoon dry sherry* |
| 3-*oz packet cream cheese* | 1 *lettuce* |
| 4 *tablespoons mayonnaise* | 4 *stuffed olives* |
| 4 *spring onions* | |

In the morning cut each avocado in halves lengthwise and remove stones. Carefully scoop out the flesh with a teaspoon, being careful not to pierce the skin. Brush over the inside of each avocado with lemon juice to prevent discolouring, and wrap in plastic bags or put into a plastic box and store in refrigerator. Mash the pulp from avocados with a fork. Soften the cream cheese with the mayonnaise and blend with the avocado pulp, add finely chopped onions, salt and pepper to taste and just enough sherry to make a smooth firm consistency. Store, covered, in refrigerator until ready to serve. Wash the lettuce, drain well and place in plastic bag in refrigerator.

Just before serving place several crisp lettuce cups on four small plates. Shred remainder of lettuce as finely as possible and use to line the avocado shells. Pile the blended avocado and cream cheese mixture into the shells on top of lettuce. Garnish each one with a sliced stuffed olive, place in the lettuce cups and serve at once.

If to be served as the main course for a summer meal, peeled, chopped shrimps can be added to the blended filling, and a few whole shrimps used to garnish each filled avocado. Cold, cooked chicken, cut into small dice, can be used in the same way instead of shrimps.

## AVOCADO-CRAB COCKTAIL

This is another avocado salad which can be served as the first course for dinner, or garnished with tomato and cucumber slices and served as a luncheon salad. It is best to prepare the filling before leaving home in the morning, but it should not be marinated for more than a day.

2 *medium-size avocados*
8 *oz can crab meat (or lobster)*
½ *cup French dressing* (page 148)
1 *teaspoon tomato paste*

1 *teaspoon onion juice*
1 *cup mayonnaise*
1 *dessertspoon lemon juice*
2 *teaspoons chopped parsley*
4 *stuffed olives*

Cut avocados in halves, remove stones and carefully remove flesh without piercing the skin. Cut flesh into dice. Brush over the inside of each avocado with lemon juice, wrap and store in refrigerator. Flake the crab or lobster, removing any shell pieces, and put into covered bowl with the avocado pieces. Pour French dressing over them, cover, and store in refrigerator until needed. Mix tomato paste, onion juice, parsley and mayonnaise together and store in refrigerator.

When ready to serve fill avocado shells with the crab

mixture, cover tops with a thin coating of mayonnaise, and garnish with sliced stuffed olives. Serve on a bed of shredded lettuce.

If serving as a luncheon salad, line the avocado shells with alternate slices of peeled tomatoes and unpeeled cucumber before filling with the crab mixture, then finish as above.

## TUNA FISH AND RICE MOULD

Much of the preparation for this salad can be done the night before, ready to finish in the morning before leaving home. The finished mould can then be stored in the refrigerator until ready to serve.

½ *lb rice*
*French dressing* (page 148)
1½ *cups cooked mixed vegetables*
  (*carrots, peas, beans, celery*)
*mayonnaise*

1 *large can tuna fish*
*salt and pepper*
*canned pimento*
*watercress*

The night before cook rice in boiling salted water for about 12 minutes, or until tender, then drain and rinse under cold water until each grain is separate. Spread out on plate to dry, tossing with a fork. Cook the peas, diced carrots, celery and beans until cooked but still crisp. Chill until ready to use.

In the morning add a little French dressing to the rice, tossing until well mixed, but do not have it too moist. Add just enough mayonnaise to vegetables to bind them together. Open can of tuna, drain well and shred the fish, removing any dark skin. Divide rice into three portions. Using a plain mould or basin, brush it over with a little cooking oil. Cut strips of pimento and place them in a crossed pattern on the bottom of mould.

Put one third of the rice into the mould, pressing down smoothly, then the vegetable mixture, another layer of rice, and then the tuna fish, seasoning each layer with salt and pepper. Lastly add a layer of rice, and press the layers down to bind them together. Cover with a piece of cooking foil and store in refrigerator until ready to serve. Turn out and garnish with watercress. Serve extra mayonnaise separately.

## POTATO SALAD

Boil well-scrubbed potatoes in their skins until tender, adding salt to taste. When cooked, drain and peel, then cut into dice while still warm. Place in a bowl with chopped onion or chives, chopped parsley and enough French dressing to sprinkle all through the potatoes, tossing lightly. Put into a cool place and leave until ready to serve. This will not harm if made the night before and stored in a cold place for the flavours to blend. Add mayonnaise just before serving.

### VARIATIONS

Add chopped pickled cucumbers to the basic recipe. Or crumbled Gorgonzola or Danish Blue cheese, or cubes of Cheddar, may be added just before serving.

Or grated raw carrot and chopped red or green peppers can be added just before serving and carefully tossed with the potatoes.

Or add chopped hard-boiled egg and a few chopped well-drained anchovies.

If you have a small amount of left-over cooked chicken, cut it into shreds and toss with the potatoes.

Use the potato salad as a filling for hollowed-out tomatoes.

Add a little extra mayonnaise, mix well and press the potato mixture into an oiled ring-mould. Chill until ready to serve, then turn out on lettuce leaves and fill centre with cold, cooked peas and diced carrots.

## WALDORF SALAD

This is a salad which is best made just before serving, but a few simple preparations can be made in the morning.

2 *cups peeled, diced apples*  *mayonnaise*
*juice of a lemon*  *lettuce cups*
2 *cups diced, young celery*  *paprika*
1 *cup roughly broken walnuts*  *small bunches of grapes*
(if available)

Wash and trim the celery, and prepare the walnuts in the morning. Just before serving, peel, core and dice the apples, sprinkle them with the lemon juice to prevent discolouring. Dice the celery, using only the crisp, inner stalks. Mix celery, apples and walnuts together, adding just enough mayonnaise to bind mixture together. Arrange on lettuce cups, sprinkle lightly with paprika, and garnish with small bunches of purple grapes, if available.

A variation of this recipe is to add cubed or coarsely grated cheese to the mixture, or if any left-over chicken is available, cut into small pieces and mix in with the mayonnaise and other ingredients.

## COLE SLAW

As a change from lettuce, make use occasionally of a firm young cabbage for a salad. The cabbage can be prepared in the morning and left to chill in a plastic bag in the refrigerator. The carrot, green pepper and onion can be prepared at the same time and left to marinate in French dressing until just before serving time, when the salad is assembled.

½ *young head of cabbage*  2 *or* 3 *young carrots*
1 *medium-size white onion*  1 *teaspoon sugar*
1 *green pepper*  *French dressing* (page 148)
1 *clove of garlic* (*if liked*)  *mayonnaise*

Cut cabbage in halves, remove hard centre core and cut in halves again. Wash well in slightly salted water, drain as much as possible and store in refrigerator in a plastic bag until needed. Chop the onion; peel and grate the carrots; cut pepper in half and remove seeds and core, then cut in thin slices. Put onion, carrot, pepper and peeled chopped clove of garlic in a bowl and just cover with French dressing. Add sugar. Cover tightly and store in refrigerator.

Just before serving, shred the cabbage as finely as possible and toss with prepared vegetables and dressing. Turn into a salad bowl and serve with mayonnaise separately.

The cole slaw may be garnished with tomato wedges and radishes if liked.

## TOMATOES WITH TUNA

Tomatoes can be hollowed out and filled with a great variety of mixtures to make a main-course salad, or to serve as an accompaniment to cold meat or fish. This recipe is more suitable for a main course, or it makes a delicious hors d'oeuvre, using smaller tomatoes.

The tomatoes can be peeled or not as desired, but I prefer them peeled. They should be left in boiling water for a few seconds, until the skin cracks, then they can easily be peeled. Cut a slice from the top of each tomato, carefully scoop out the pulp, season with salt and pepper and turn upside-down to drain. Chill until ready to fill and serve.

| | |
|---|---|
| 4 *large, round tomatoes* | 10 *or* 12 *capers* |
| 1 *small can anchovies* | 1 *sweet red pepper or canned* |
| 1 *small can tuna* | *pimento* |
| 2 *hard-boiled eggs* | *salt and pepper* |
| | *mayonnaise* |

Drain anchovies and tuna and chop roughly. Chop the capers and red pepper or pimento and add to mayonnaise. Slice the eggs, retaining 4 perfect slices, and chop remainder, adding to fish. Mix fish and mayonnaise mixtures together and taste for seasoning, being careful not to have the mixture too moist. Fill tomatoes with this, place an egg slice on top of each one, and serve at once, with extra mayonnaise if liked.

## QUICK-FILLED TOMATOES

Other fillings for hollowed-out tomatoes which can be quickly and easily prepared:

Canned sweet corn mixed with a little mayonnaise or salad dressing, and the well-drained pulp from the tomatoes.

Cooked peas seasoned with chopped chives or finely chopped onion and a little French dressing (page 148).

Cooked rice tossed with grated raw carrot, chopped celery and chopped chives, and moistened with a little French dressing.

Cooked macaroni, tossed with a little mayonnaise and grated cheese. Season well with a little cayenne or curry powder.

All these can be served on lettuce leaves, or ringed with Cole Slaw (page 132) and served on individual plates.

## MOULDED VEGETABLES

Prepare these individual moulds the night before and leave to chill and set in refrigerator until ready to serve. They are a good way of using up vegetables cooked and left from the previous dinner. The best vegetables are diced carrots, diced French beans, peas, diced celery, and diced green and red peppers can also be added. If more convenient, canned mixed vegetables can be used.

| | |
|---|---|
| 1 *packet of lemon jelly* | 1 *teaspoon finely chopped parsley* |
| ½ *teaspoon salt* | 1½ *cups diced, cooked vegetables* |
| 2 *teaspoons grated onion* | *lettuce cups* |
| 1 *tablespoon white vinegar* | |

Dissolve jelly in 1¾ cups hot water. Add salt, vinegar and grated onion, chill until slightly thickened, then add cooked vegetables and parsley. Turn into 4 small moulds and chill until firm.

When ready to serve, turn moulds out on to lettuce cups. Pass mayonnaise separately. If preferred, this mixture can be moulded in one larger mould or ring shape. If a ring shape is used, fill centre with peeled and chopped tomatoes.


## ORANGE SALAD VALENCIA

A quickly and easily prepared salad which makes a colourful addition to a cold meat or fish plate.

| | |
|---|---|
| 4 *large, juicy oranges* | 1 *tablespoon olive oil* |
| 1 *small onion, or chopped chives* | 1 *tablespoon lemon juice* |
| 6 *or* 8 *black olives* | *salt and pepper* |

Peel oranges, carefully removing all the white pith. Cut in crosswise slices, about ½-inch thick. Peel and chop onion very fine, or chop chives, and sprinkle over oranges. Cut olives in halves and remove stones, then cut in strips and use to garnish orange slices. Mix lemon juice, oil, salt and pepper and pour over oranges. Serve at once.

# SIMPLE CUCUMBER AND TOMATO SALAD

A very simple salad to serve with cold meat or canned fish. The cucumber should be prepared before leaving home in the morning, and the tomatoes can be peeled and left to chill.

1 *young cucumber*
*salt and pepper*
1 *teaspoon sugar*
1 *teaspoon finely chopped mint*

1 *tablespoon tarragon vinegar*
3 *or* 4 *peeled tomatoes*
*mayonnaise or dressing*

Peel cucumber and cut into thin slices. Put into a basin with salt, pepper and sugar and sprinkle with mint, tossing to mix well. Add the vinegar, and allow to stand in a cool place.

When ready to serve drain cucumber well. Slice the tomatoes and place alternate rows of tomato slices and cucumber on a serving plate. Season with salt and pepper, and serve mayonnaise or salad dressing separately.

# GRECIAN CUCUMBER SALAD

The ingredients for this unusual and very tasty salad are best prepared in the morning before leaving home, then assembled just before serving. This mixture makes a good addition to cold meat or accompanied by cold salmon or tuna, or it can be served as an hors d'oeuvre.

1 *young cucumber*
½ *pint yoghurt*
1 *small clove of garlic*
1 *dessertspoon olive oil*
1 *dessertspoon vinegar*

6 *or* 8 *black olives*
½ *oz shelled walnuts*
*salt and pepper*
*lettuce*

Peel cucumber and coarsely grate into a soup plate. Sprinkle with salt, cover with another plate and leave in a cool place to extract the water. Peel and crush the garlic with a little salt and mix with oil and vinegar, then blend this into yoghurt, mixing well. Cover and chill. Chop the walnuts; halve and stone the olives, and cut into strips.

When ready to serve mix well-drained cucumber, the olives and walnuts to yoghurt, and pile on lettuce leaves.

## RICE AND SEA FOOD SALAD

The rice and peas in this salad are cooked the night before and chilled ready for serving next day.

½ *lb long-grain rice*
1½ *cups cooked peas*
1 *can (5 oz) pimentoes or 1 sweet red pepper*
1 *can anchovy fillets*
½ *lb peeled prawns or shrimps*
½ *teaspoon grated lemon rind*
*juice of 1 lemon*
*sprinkle of paprika*
*French dressing* (page 148)
*lettuce*
*mayonnaise*

When ready to serve, drain and chop pimentoes, or if using fresh peppers, remove seeds and core and chop. Slice anchovies in halves, lengthwise, and drain well. Line a salad bowl with lettuce leaves, first rubbing round with a cut clove of garlic.

Toss together the rice, peas, lemon rind, pimentoes or red pepper, prawns or shrimps and lemon juice. Pile into the prepared salad bowl, sprinkle lightly with paprika and garnish with anchovy fillets.

## MUSHROOMS VINAIGRETTE

This is a delicious recipe which can be served as a salad or as

E*                    137

an hors d'oeuvre. It should be prepared the night before and left to stand in the marinade until ready to serve.

1 *lb small mushrooms*
*salt and pepper*
1 *dessertspoon finely chopped chives*
1 *clove of garlic (if liked)*

1 *dessertspoon finely chopped parsley*
2 *tablespoons malt vinegar*
*chicory*
*French dressing* (page 148)

Wipe mushrooms but do not peel, remove stems, place mushrooms in saucepan with peeled clove of garlic, salt and pepper and boiling water just to cover. Simmer quietly until mushrooms are tender. Drain well and place in deep bowl, removing the garlic. Sprinkle with chives and parsley and add vinegar, tossing until well mixed. Cover and place in refrigerator until ready to serve.

Drain mushrooms well and place in serving bowl with chicory leaves (or lettuce), adding a little French dressing and serving remainder separately.

## ASPARAGUS AND FRENCH BEAN SALAD

An excellent salad to use up the extra French beans from last night's cooking. Either freshly cooked or canned asparagus tips can be used.

12 *asparagus tips*
½ *lb cooked French beans*
3 *or* 4 *peeled tomatoes*
½ *lb liver sausage*

*lettuce*
*bunch of watercress*
¼ *pint mayonnaise*
2 *tablespoons sweet stout*

Line a serving dish with lettuce leaves. Cut tomatoes into quarters, cut beans into 1-inch pieces, lightly mixing with tomatoes. Heap in the middle of the dish and lightly coat with mayonnaise to which you have added the stout. Arrange sliced liver sausage (any other similar sausage such as salami may be used if preferred) and asparagus tips around the tomato-bean mixture. Garnish with watercress.

Serve remaining mayonnaise mixture separately.

# Sauces and Dressings

A quickly made sauce, or one which can be made up in quantity and stored in the refrigerator until needed, can be a great boon to the busy housewife. Simple foods can gain new importance with a good sauce, and a plain salad can make a meal when well dressed with one of the mayonnaise or salad dressings given in this chapter.

For a meal in a hurry, flake a can of salmon into ½ pint of plain white sauce, turn into a casserole and sprinkle top with grated cheese or browned breadcrumbs, and heat in the oven until bubbling and golden brown on top – and you have a meal.

Or hard-boil some eggs, heat up the curry sauce you have in the refrigerator and serve over the shelled eggs set in a bed of freshly cooked rice – all done in under half an hour.

But why go on – the possibilities are numerous, and you will be able to think of many more to suit your needs and your taste. And the sauces given here are only a few of those which can be added to your culinary lists, I have chosen them as being probably the most useful.

And we must not forget the sweet sauces, which can be served over a block of ice cream bought on your way home and then glamorized for a special dessert with a sauce such as the Chocolate Peppermint or the Hot Toddy sauces given here. Or serve the Banana-Ginger Cream over canned pineapple slices, or Ruby Sauce over canned peaches for family or special guests.

# BASIC WHITE SAUCES

There are many uses for a simple white sauce, or béchamel as it should properly be called, and it is very easy to make. You can make up double quantities at a time and store the surplus in the refrigerator in a covered container. It can be re-heated over hot water, and the required seasoning added as it heats. If serving with fish, half fish stock can be used instead of all milk; for chicken use half chicken stock and half milk and add a spoonful of cream when sauce is cooked.

| | |
|---|---|
| 1 *oz butter* | ½ *pint hot milk* |
| 1 *oz flour* | *salt and pepper to taste* |

Melt butter in a small saucepan then blend in the flour until well mixed, and cook for 2 or 3 minutes without allowing to brown (this is known as a roux). Remove pan from heat and gradually stir in the milk, a little at a time, making sure there are no lumps (a wire whisk is good for this). The sauce is returned to the heat and stirred until thickened, then cooked gently for a few minutes. Add the seasoning as required.

If a brown sauce is wanted, cook the flour in the butter for longer, until it is browned, and use beef bouillon instead of milk. Make the bouillon with a cube if necessary.

# SAUCE MEUNIÈRE

Simple and delicious, this is excellent over grilled fish, on grilled steak and over hot asparagus.

In a thick, small saucepan heat 2 oz butter until it is light brown and has the aroma of toasted nuts. Add 1 dessertspoon lemon juice and ½ teaspoon finely chopped parsley. Serve at once.

## SAUCE AMANDINE

Also excellent with grilled fish. Make as above but instead of parsley add 1 tablespoon shredded blanched almonds.

## MORNAY SAUCE

Make up basic béchamel sauce and add 1 tablespoon each of grated Parmesan cheese and grated Gruyère cheese (or Cheddar may be used if preferred). Stir well until cheese melts, then remove from heat and stir in 1 tablespoon thick cream.

## SOUBISE SAUCE

This is simply the addition of cooked onions to the basic white sauce. To ½ pint of sauce allow ½ lb onions, peeled and chopped small, then cooked in two tablespoons of water until soft, shaking frequently to prevent burning. Then add a tablespoon of butter, salt and pepper to taste, and stir until the butter is absorbed. Press through a sieve into the warm white sauce and heat together over hot water.

## SAUCE PROVENÇAL

A useful sauce to serve over fish or over roast meat instead of gravy. It can be made the day before using, stored in a covered jar in refrigerator, and re-heated just before serving.

| | |
|---|---|
| 1 *oz butter* | ½ *lb tomatoes, peeled* |
| 1 *tablespoon olive or maize oil* | 1 *clove of garlic (if liked)* |
| 1 *sweet red pepper* | *salt and pepper to taste* |

Cut top from red pepper and remove seeds, then cut in strips. Roughly chop the tomatoes. Heat butter and oil together in a saucepan and add garlic, leaving until it is lightly browned, then remove and discard. Add pepper and tomatoes and simmer for 25 minutes, covered. Put through a sieve and season to taste. Store overnight, then re-heat when needed.

# QUICK CUMBERLAND SAUCE

Serve this cold with cold duck or ham, or heat it over hot water for wild duck or other game birds.

3 *tablespoons red currant jelly*  1 *wineglass of sherry*
1 *tablespoon orange marmalade*  *pinch cayenne*
1 *tablespoon lemon juice*  1 *teaspoon mixed mustard*

Blend all ingredients together and serve hot or cold.

# CURRY SAUCE

With a good curry sauce you are never at a loss for a quick meal, as the sauce can be served over canned meat or fish; over left-over meat or hard-boiled eggs, or even over a mixture of cooked vegetables. It is best served with freshly boiled rice, but I have served curry with cooked macaroni or mashed potatoes on occasion.

The sauce can be made up overnight, then re-heated just before serving. If serving with left-over or canned meat, it is best to heat the meat up in the sauce. Side dishes of peanuts, coconut, chutney, lemon wedges or diced pineapple can be served with the curry.

2 *medium size onions, chopped*
1 *clove of garlic (if liked)*
2 *oz bacon fat or dripping*
1 *tablespoon curry powder (or to taste)*
1 *bay leaf*
1 *tablespoon flour*

*salt and pepper*
1 *apple, chopped*
½ *lb tomatoes or small can of tomatoes*
*seeded raisins or sultanas*
½ *pint stock or water*

Fry the onions and finely chopped garlic in the fat until soft. Sprinkle with the curry powder and flour and blend in well, cooking for a few minutes, then stir in stock or water. Add remainder of ingredients and simmer covered, for 30 minutes, stirring occasionally. Add more stock or water if sauce is too thick. If a smoother sauce is wanted, put it through a sieve or into an electric blender.

If making up a curry dish with uncooked meat, add it to the sauce after sieving, and simmer until cooked. It will improve with storing overnight.


## SWEET AND SOUR SAUCE

A useful sauce to serve over poached or grilled fish (frozen fish fingers are useful here), or it is tasty over pork chops or fillets. The vegetables can be prepared in the morning or overnight and stored in a plastic bag in the refrigerator. If using poached fish, the fish stock can be used in the sauce, or with pork make stock with a bouillon or chicken cube.

1 *medium onion*
1 *medium carrot*
1 *stalk of celery*
*salt and pepper*

1½ *tablespoons sugar*
½ *cup vinegar*
1 *cup fish or meat stock*
1 *tablespoon cornflour*

Grate the carrot, chop the celery and onion. Add to stock

with the sugar and simmer together for 5 minutes. Blend the cornflour into a cream with the vinegar and stir into vegetables, stirring until thickened. Taste for seasoning, remembering that stock has already been salted.

## MINT AND HONEY SAUCE

If you have mint growing in your garden, make up a quantity of this sauce to last through the winter. Serve it with roast lamb or lamb chops and green peas. It should be warmed before serving – nothing is worse than cold mint sauce over hot meat.

| | |
|---|---|
| 1 *cup finely chopped mint* | ½ *cup vinegar* |
| ½ *cup honey* | ½ *cup water* |
| *pinch salt* | |

When measuring mint, press it down firmly into cup. Put honey, vinegar and water into saucepan and heat slowly until honey is dissolved, stirring constantly. Let it come to the boil, then simmer for 5 minutes, covered. Cool slightly and pour over mint. Season to taste. Put into two small jars with screw tops, and use as required. It can be thinned down with water or vinegar as required.

## ORANGE-MINT SAUCE

For a new flavour with lamb, try making mint and orange sauce by using half orange juice and half vinegar with freshly chopped mint. Add sugar to taste and ½ teaspoon grated orange rind. Allow to steep in a warm place for at least 30 minutes before serving.

# SEASONED BUTTERS

Instead of a sauce to serve with fish, meat or vegetables you may prefer seasoned butter, which can be prepared overnight and left in refrigerator to harden before serving.

Any of these seasoned butters can also be used as a spread for savoury biscuits or canapés. Unsalted butter is preferred, and the butter should be slightly softened but *not* melted before working in the additions.

To 4 oz butter blend in a choice of the following ingredients:

*Anchovy Butter:* 6 drained anchovy fillets, chopped small and blended with a fork before adding to butter. Good with plain grilled fish fillets or with veal chops or veal escalopes.

*Lemon Butter:* 1 tablespoon lemon juice and 1 teaspoon finely grated lemon rind. For grilled or fried fish, or as a spread with shrimp or prawn canapés.

*Maître d'Hotel Butter:* 1 tablespoon finely chopped parsley and juice of ½ lemon. A scraping of onion may also be used if liked. For grilled steak, game and some vegetables such as asparagus or broccoli.

*Bercy Butter:* As above, but use chopped chives instead of parsley, and omit the onion.

*Mustard Butter:* 1 tablespoon mixed mustard and 2 or 3 drops of Worcestershire sauce. For ham, beef or veal.

# MAYONNAISE

Mayonnaise is probably the most popular of cold sauces, and can be served not only with salads but also with fish and vegetable dishes. It can be made in quantity and stored in the refrigerator, but excessive cold will cause the mayonnaise to separate, so remove for a little time before serving and shake well. If you have someone in the kitchen while you are making the mayonnaise, get them to drip the oil into the mixture as you beat it. This reduces the risk of curdling. But if you beat the mixture steadily and add oil very slowly in the beginning you should not have any trouble.

If by some mischance it does curdle, beat up another egg yolk in a clean basin and gradually beat in the curdled mayonnaise, a spoonful at a time, until it has all been absorbed into the fresh yolk.

| | |
|---|---|
| 2 *egg yolks* | *freshly ground pepper* |
| 1 *teaspoon dry mustard* | 2 *tablespoons vinegar or lemon* |
| ½ *teaspoon salt* | *juice* |
| ½ *teaspoon sugar* | 2 *cups olive oil* |
| 1 *clove of garlic (if liked)* | 1 *dessertspoon boiling water* |

Beat the egg yolks well, then add mustard, sugar, salt and pepper and vinegar or lemon juice, and beat to mix well. Continue beating while adding the oil, almost drop by drop at first, then as the mixture thickens increase the flow of oil until it has all been absorbed, beating continually all the time. If the mayonnaise is to be kept for a time, beat in the boiling water at the very end of the beating.

If you like the flavour of garlic, cut the clove in halves and rub round the bowl in which you are to make the mayonnaise.

Using mayonnaise as a base, there are a number of delicious sauces which can add flavour to simple meals, and are very useful in an emergency:

*Sauce Andalouse :* Add 3 or 4 tablespoons tomato purée, ½ teaspoon sugar, and sweet red pepper or canned pimento cut into thin strips.

*Cucumber Sauce :* Add ½ cup peeled and chopped cucumber and 2 tablespoons finely chopped chives to 1 cup of mayonnaise. Stand for half an hour then serve with any fish salad.

*Piquant Tomato Mayonnaise :* To 1 cup mayonnaise add 2 tablespoons tomato paste, 2 tablespoons sweet stout, 2 teaspoons lemon juice, ½ teaspoon Worcestershire sauce and 2 teaspoons sugar. Mix well and stand for half an hour, then add some finely chopped parsley or chives before serving.

## YOGHURT DRESSING

For those on a slimming diet, this dressing will be welcomed.
Use it to add flavour to a simple lettuce and tomato salad.

1 *cup yoghurt*  
2 *teaspoons lemon juice*  

½ *teaspoon salt*  
1 *dessertspoon finely chopped chives or parsley*

Beat all together and chill for at least an hour before
serving.

Another variation of this is to add the yolks of two hard-
boiled eggs to the yoghurt, mashing them well together then
add remainder of ingredients, increasing the amount of
lemon juice if too thick.

## TARTARE SAUCE IN LEMON CUPS

This is a simple version of a very popular sauce for fish.

1 *cup mayonnaise*  
2 *teaspoons chopped capers*  
2 *teaspoons chopped gherkins*  

1 *teaspoon onion juice*  
*paprika*  
*shells of 4 lemon halves*

Use lemon halves from which juice has been squeezed as
containers for the sauce. Scoop out any pulp remaining, and
cut a small slice from the bottom to make the halves sit
firmly. Mix remainder of ingredients to mayonnaise and
serve in lettuce cups.

## FRENCH DRESSING

This dressing can be made up in quantity and kept in a
covered jar in a cool place, but not in the refrigerator. More

or less oil can be used as desired, and either olive oil or corn oil can be used. All vinegar can be used if preferred.

| | |
|---|---|
| 2 *tablespoons olive oil* | ¼ *teaspoon sugar* |
| 1 *tablespoon vinegar* | *salt and pepper to taste* |
| 1 *dessertspoon lemon juice* | 1 *small clove of garlic* |
| ¼ *teaspoon dry mustard* | |

Mash the garlic in the bottom of a bowl with the sugar, mustard, salt and pepper, using the back of a wooden spoon. Blend in lemon juice and vinegar, then slowly add the oil, mixing well. Use over lettuce or other salad greens, tossing the leaves to coat evenly with the dressing. Serve at once.

## SAUCES FOR ICE CREAM

A block of plain ice cream gains an air of importance if served with a well-flavoured and colourful sauce. A hot sauce poured over well-frozen ice cream immediately before serving is a delightful contrast, or cold fruit sauces are delicious on a warm day.

*Caramel-Coffee Sauce:* ¼ lb caramels, 2 tablespoons top milk, 1 teaspoon instant coffee.

Use a small, thick saucepan. Put caramels and top milk into the pan and stir over low heat until dissolved. Stir in the instant coffee (use a little extra if a strong coffee flavour is wanted) until well blended. This may be served hot or cold.

*Chocolate-Peppermint Sauce:* 4 oz chocolate peppermint creams, 3 tablespoons cream. Break peppermint creams in halves and put into a small basin, which will stand in a saucepan of gently boiling water. Stir occasionally until creams have melted, then stir in cream and stir until smooth. Serve hot or cold.

*Ruby Sauce:* 1 cup apple or redcurrant jelly, 2 tablespoons claret or Burgundy wine.

Heat jelly in a basin over hot water until softened but not melted. Add wine and beat with a fork, keeping the rough appearance. Serve at once over ice cream.

## BANANA-GINGER CREAM

This is a quickly made sauce which should be served at once, as the bananas tend to discolour if kept for any time. Serve it over chocolate ice cream, or over slices of canned pineapple or pears.

| | |
|---|---|
| 4 *firm but ripe bananas* | ½ *pint whipping cream* |
| 1 *oz crystallized ginger, chopped* | *sugar to taste* |
| 2 *teaspoons lemon juice* | |

Peel bananas and remove the 'threads', then mash with a fork until quite smooth and free from lumps, adding the lemon juice and sugar to taste. Whip the cream until thick but not stiff, fold in the bananas and the finely chopped ginger.

The mixture should be the consistency of a thick pouring sauce.

## APRICOT AND ORANGE SAUCE

Another quickly made sauce to be served hot or cold.

| | |
|---|---|
| ½ *cup apricot jam* | 1 *teaspoon grated orange rind* |
| ¼ *cup orange juice* | 2 *tablespoons rum or brandy* |

Combine jam, juice and orange rind and heat slowly, stirring until blended. Remove from heat and stir in rum or brandy. Serve hot over ice cream or custard, or chill in refrigerator until needed next day.

# SPICED APPLE-ORANGE SAUCE

Well chilled, this makes a delicious sauce over ice cream, or hot it can be served over plain baked custard or a steamed pudding. For the children, make sundaes by putting alternate spoonfuls of chilled apple sauce and ice cream into tall glasses.

The sauce improves with keeping for at least 12 hours before serving, as the flavours blend together better.

| | |
|---|---|
| 1 *lb cooking apples* | ½ *teaspoon ground cinnamon* |
| 1 *large orange* | ½ *teaspoon ground ginger* |
| ½ *lemon* | ¼ *teaspoon ground nutmeg, or use* |
| 1 *tablespoon honey* | 1 *teaspoon ground mixed spice* |
| 1 *tablespoon sugar* | |

Wash the orange, grate the rind (be careful not to include any of the white pith) and squeeze out the juice. Grate the rind from the half-lemon and squeeze out the juice. Put cored, peeled and sliced apples into a covered saucepan with the orange and lemon juice, and cook gently until apples are soft and mushy. Beat until smooth and free from lumps, then add remainder of ingredients and boil together for 1 minute. Taste to see if sweet enough. Some apples are more juicy than others, so if the sauce is too thick, add a little more orange juice. Cool and chill until ready to serve.

# HOT TODDY SAUCE

Try this well-flavoured sauce served hot over ice cream, or for an emergency dessert pour it over slices of plain cake and add a spoonful of cream to each serve. The sauce will keep in a covered jar in the refrigerator for several days after making, needing only to be heated up over hot water.

3 *tablespoons golden syrup*
1 *dessertspoon cornflour*
¼ *pint water*
*juice of* 1 *lemon*
2 *tablespoons rum or sweet sherry*
 *or* 2 *tablespoons orange juice*

1 *tablespoon blanched and*
 *chopped almonds*
1 *tablespoon chopped glacé*
 *cherries*
1 *tablespoon chopped, seeded*
 *raisins*

Soak the chopped cherries and raisins in the rum or sherry, or orange juice if preferred, for an hour before making the sauce. Heat the syrup in a small, thick saucepan until lightly caramelized. Remove from heat and stir in water gradually. Blend cornflour and lemon juice together and add to caramel liquid, then stir over low heat until boiling, stirring for several more minutes as it simmers. Cool slightly and add remainder of ingredients, re-heating if necessary but do not allow to boil again.

# Luncheon and Supper Dishes

Included in this chapter are many recipes which you may also find suitable for dinner, but they are not as substantial as those in the meat and poultry chapters.

Some of the dishes could be served as the first course for a special dinner, others are suitable for a meatless meal when accompanied by vegetables, while others would be ideal for taking on a picnic over the week-end.

There are dishes which can be prepared, cooked and served in half an hour, others which need some preparation done the night before, but all are easy enough for the cook who comes home tired after a hard day's work, and wants only a light meal.

## ASPARAGUS AND HAM BUNDLES

This is a very versatile recipe and can be served hot or cold, as a salad or with an hors d'oeuvre plate, or hot for a luncheon dish. Providing you have the ingredients on hand it can be prepared and served in a few minutes, using canned asparagus, or if using fresh asparagus, it will need to be cooked the night before.

Allow 4 sticks of asparagus to each thin slice of ham. Wrap the well drained tips in the ham and fasten securely with wooden cocktail sticks. Arrange in a buttered ovenproof dish, in a single layer if possible, pour 3 or 4 tablespoons thick cream over the top and sprinkle thickly with grated Parmesan cheese. Dot with small pieces of butter and put into a moderately hot oven (400° F or No 5–6) for 6 to 8 minutes, until cheese and butter have melted and ham is lightly tinted. Serve at once.

If serving cold, prepare the bundles and arrange on lettuce leaves, then serve with mayonnaise.

Another variation is to cover the prepared bundles with Mornay Sauce (page 142) and put under the griller or in the oven until bubbling and lightly browned on top.

## GOLDEN POTATO EGGS

These make a tasty lunch dish, or they are excellent to pack cold for a picnic meal. All the preparations can be done the night before, ready to be cooked just before serving if a hot meal is wanted, or they can be cooked and served cold next day with salad.

| | |
|---|---|
| 1½ *lb mashed potatoes* | 3 *oz grated tasty cheese* |
| 6 *hard-boiled eggs* | 1 *beaten egg* |
| 6 *spring onions, chopped* | *browned breadcrumbs* |
| *salt and pepper* | *deep fat for frying* |

Shell and chop the hard-boiled eggs. Chop the onions (or substitute 1 tablespoon finely chopped parsley, if preferred) and mix with the cheese and eggs into the smoothly mashed potatoes. Season to taste and mould the mixture into the shape of eggs. Allow to stand in refrigerator for 15 minutes. Dip each egg-shape into beaten egg, then coat with breadcrumbs, making sure they are coated evenly all over. Deep-fry in hot fat until golden brown. Drain on absorbent paper.

If serving hot, they look nice set in nests of cooked string beans, or set on a thick slice of tomato, which has been grilled while the eggs are frying.

## CRAB AND SCRAMBLED EGGS

This is a very quick and easy supper dish, served on rounds of toast.

| | |
|---|---|
| 1 *small can of crab* | *salt and pepper* |
| 6 *eggs* | *paprika* |
| 2 *tablespoons top milk* | *butter* |
| | 4 *slices buttered toast* |

Drain the crab and remove any hard pieces, then flake into small pieces. Beat the eggs with a fork until light and frothy, add top milk, salt and pepper and fold in the crab meat. Melt a dessertspoon butter in a thick pan and pour in the egg mixture. Leave for a few minutes until setting round the edges, then stir into the centre with the fork, continuing to do this until mixture is just setting all over. Remove from heat and divide mixture between the four pieces of toast. Dust top over with paprika and serve at once. Care should be taken not to overcook the eggs.

## HAM AND ASPARAGUS BAKE

Canned condensed soups make very useful sauces and add flavour to simple dishes. This recipe is a good way of using up cooked rice to make tomorrow's lunch or hot supper. If you have some cold, cooked chicken or veal it can be used instead of ham.

| | |
|---|---|
| 2 *cups diced, cooked ham* | 1 *large can cream of asparagus* |
| 2 *cups cooked rice* | *soup* |
| ½ *cup grated cheese* | 2 *tablespoons grated onion* |
| ½ *cup top milk or evaporated milk* | ¾ *cup cornflake crumbs* |
| | 2 *tablespoons melted butter* |

Mix the rice, ham, cheese, onion, top milk and soup, and pour into a greased ovenproof dish. Toss the cornflake crumbs in the melted butter and sprinkle over top of rice mixture. Bake in a moderate oven (350° F or No 5) until bubbling hot and the top crisp and lightly browned. Serve at once.

## CHICKEN LIVERS IN PEPPER CASES

These ingredients can be prepared the night before, ready to be put together and baked for 10 minutes just before serving.

½ *lb chicken livers*      4 *oz lean bacon rashers*
1 *cup cooked rice*       *salt and pepper*
1 *large onion*           4 *sweet red peppers*
2 *oz butter*

Choose 4 peppers of a nice shape for stuffing, all the same size if possible. Blanche them first by putting into a saucepan of salted water and bringing to the boil, boil for 2 minutes then drain. Cut off the tops and carefully remove the seeds and membranes inside. Chop the bacon and fry in a little butter with the sliced onion and chicken livers, stirring to cook evenly. After 2 or 3 minutes, stir in rice and blend all together in the pan. Season with salt and pepper to taste, then spoon the rice filling into the peppers. Pack the filled peppers into a greased ovenproof dish so that they stand firmly upright, cover with a piece of buttered paper and bake in a moderate oven for 10 minutes or until heated through.

Baked, halved tomatoes, sprinkled with chopped chives and baked alongside the peppers are good with this.

## MEXICAN CASSEROLE

This simple casserole can be prepared and cooked in 30 minutes, or it can be prepared in the morning before leaving home, and put into the oven to cook for 20 minutes before serving.

It could also be served as a vegetable course for dinner if desired.

| | |
|---|---|
| 4 *large ripe tomatoes, peeled* | 3 *or* 4 *rashers bacon* |
| 12-*oz can of sweet corn* | *salt and pepper* |
| 2 *onions, sliced* | *pinch sugar* |
| 1 *sweet red pepper* | *butter or margarine* |
| 1 *dessertspoon chopped parsley* | 1 *packet potato crisps* |

Wash red pepper, remove seeds and chop small. Slice the tomatoes about ¼-inch thick, chop the bacon pieces. Melt a little butter or margarine in a pan and fry the bacon until crisp. Remove from pan and drain on paper. Sauté the onions and pepper in the fat in pan, adding a little more fat if necessary, until onions are tender but not browned. Spread the onion mixture on the bottom of a greased casserole, cover with well-drained sweet corn, sprinkle with parsley and the bacon pieces, and season to taste. Cover with sliced tomatoes, sprinkle with salt, pepper and sugar, and the finely crushed potato crisps. Dot with a few pieces of butter and bake in a moderately hot oven (375° F or No 5) for 20 minutes.

## EGG AND ONION CASSEROLE

All the preparations for this casserole can be done the night before, and it will only need to be put together and baked for 20 minutes before serving. Served with a green vegetable it would be substantial enough for a main course for a light meatless meal.

| | |
|---|---|
| 6 *or* 8 *hard-boiled eggs* | 2 *oz butter or margarine* |
| 3 *large onions* | 2 *oz flour* |
| 4 *oz cooked rice* | 1 *pint milk* |
| 1 *tablespoon chopped parsley or* | *salt and pepper to taste* |
| *celery leaves* | 3 *oz grated cheese* |

Cook the eggs and the rice. Slice the onions and cook in the butter or margarine until soft but not browned. Blend in the flour until absorbed in the butter, then slowly stir in the warmed milk, stirring until sauce thickens. Add salt, pepper and parsley and cook for two or three minutes. Cool and store in a covered container in refrigerator until next day. Warm the sauce over boiling water. Slice the eggs, and arrange alternate layers of rice, sliced eggs and onion sauce in a greased casserole, finishing with a layer of sauce. Sprinkle top with grated cheese and bake in a moderate oven (350° F or No 4) until mixture bubbles with heat and is golden on top.

## OMELETTES

An omelette is a busy cook's best friend, as with eggs in the larder you can always produce a tasty meal for your family or unexpected guests in quick time.

You can serve an omelette for breakfast, luncheon or even dinner – but please, not on the same day. You can stretch an omelette by adding a filling of asparagus tips or salmon from the larder, or you can make an omelette for dessert with a filling of chopped canned fruit, or with a sauce such as the apricot and orange on page 150.

So invest in an omelette pan (one with a good thick base and gently sloping sides) and keep it just for omelettes, making sure the family know it is not to be used for anything else, except perhaps crêpes or pancakes.

There are two main types of omelette, the French and the

soufflé or 'puffy' type. Dessert omelettes are usually made like a soufflé omelette, with a fruity filling. Another type is the Spanish omelette, with basically the same ingredients as the French, but cooked in a different manner.

## FRENCH OMELETTE

If you prefer to make individual omelettes (in my opinion you cannot successfully serve more than three individual omelettes at a meal and still sit down to eat with the family), choose a pan 7 or 8 inches across. If you want to make large omelettes to serve 3 people at once, choose a 9- to 10-inch pan.

Small omelettes require 2 or 3 eggs and the larger ones need 6 eggs. For each egg allow 1 teaspoon of water, salt and pepper, and any flavourings such as chopped parsley of chives, a dash of Worcestershire sauce or a sprinkle or paprika. Melt a good dessertspoon of butter in a small pan, or a tablespoon in the larger pan, so that when melted you have a thin film of butter all over the bottom and sides of the pan. Cooking oil can be used instead of butter if preferred.

Break eggs into a bowl, add water and seasonings and beat with a fork just until well mixed. Do not over-beat or it will be heavy. When butter sizzles and foams (on no account allow it to brown) pour in the egg mixture quickly. It should begin to set round the edges almost at once. With a thin-bladed spatula lift the omelette up round the edges, tilting the pan so that the uncooked part runs over into the pan. This gives the rippled surface and irregular edges characteristic of a good omelette. It is cooked when the egg no longer runs freely, but is still slightly creamy on top. If filling is to be added, now is the time, placing the filling on one half only, the side farthest away from you.

Hold the pan over a warmed plate and slide the omelette on to it, giving it a twist to fold other half on top of the filling. Serve at once. If you want to keep omelettes hot while you make others, put on the plate over a saucepan of hot water rather than in the oven, but work as quickly as possible or they will toughen.

Add 1 tablespoon grated cheese to egg mixture before cooking, with a pinch of dry mustard.

Grill 2 slices lean bacon until crisp, then crumble and add to egg mixture just as it is setting.

Sauté ¼ lb chopped mushrooms in butter, and after placing cooked omelette on heated plate, pour the cooked mushrooms over half the omelette, folding other half over the mushrooms. Serve at once.

Chopped, left-over chicken pieces can be added to a Mornay Sauce (page 142) and used as a filling after omelette is removed from pan to plate; or shrimps or chopped crab meat can be used in place of chicken. Add a spoonful of sherry to the sauce for a special dish.

## SOUFFLE OMELETTE

As its name indicates, a soufflé omelette should puff up while cooking, and unlike the French type, it is beaten well to get a light consistency.

Using a small pan, a soufflé omelette will give two serves, and for a more substantial dish a savoury filling can be added just before serving. The filling should be prepared and cooked before beginning the omelette, as speed is essential to keep the omelette light.

To serve 2 take 4 eggs, 1 tablespoon milk, salt and pepper and 1 dessertspoon butter. Melt the butter and swirl round pan to coat bottom and sides, but do not let it brown.

Separate the yolks and whites of the eggs. Beat whites until they form peaks. Beat yolks with the salt and pepper until thick, then add milk. Fold whites into yolks and pour at once into buttered pan, spreading mixture evenly. Cook over low heat until omelette puffs up and underpart is set and lightly golden. If it shows any signs of sticking to the pan, lift up slightly and add more butter. When cooked on the bottom, put under heated griller until top is slightly dry and springs back when pressed lightly with a fingertip. Slip carefully on to a hot plate, and with the back of a knife draw a line across the middle and fold over.

Any fillings can be added just before folding over.

## CHINESE OMELETTE

Either chopped, cooked chicken or cooked prawns or shrimps can be used for this, which is made to serve 2 or 3, using the large-size omelette pan.

| | |
|---|---|
| 6 *eggs* | ½ *cup finely chopped shallots or* |
| *salt and pepper* | *white onions* |
| 1 *tablespoon water* | 4 *to* 6 *oz chopped, shredded* |
| 1 *tablespoon butter or oil* | *chicken or shelled prawns or* |
| ¼ *lb mushrooms, sliced thin* | *shrimps* |

Heat the butter or oil in pan and sauté the shallots and mushrooms until cooked. Add chicken or prawns and heat through, then pour over the beaten egg mixture. Cook as directed for French omelette. Fold over and serve at once when cooked. Serve with soya sauce.

## SPANISH OMELETTE

A Spanish omelette is made with the same basic ingredients as the French one, but it is served flat, and cooked on both sides. When the omelette is golden underneath, it is carefully turned over in the pan and cooked on the other side.

Instead of folding over a filling, the ingredients are cooked in with the egg, or else served as a sauce over the plain omelette.

Cooked, sliced potatoes, peeled chopped tomatoes, and lightly cooked, sliced onions can be added to the egg mixture, and oil is used instead of butter to grease the pan.

Sauce Provençal (page 142) is good to serve over a Spanish omelette in which sliced potatoes and onions have been cooked, or over a plain omelette.

## CHICKEN AND MUSHROOM CREPES

We are too often inclined to think of pancakes or crêpes only as a dessert course, to be served with sugar and lemon wedges, or with jam; but a seasoned batter made up into paper-thin pancakes, then rolled round a savoury filling, can make a delicious meal.

The crêpes can be prepared the night before, if necessary, then wrapped in foil or in an airtight container in the refrigerator until just before serving time. The filling can also be prepared the night before, and there is a wide choice of suitable mixtures which are easy to prepare and which do not harm with keeping, many depending on left-overs you may have on hand, such as chicken pieces, and vegetables.

BASIC BATTER

*4 oz plain flour*  
*pinch salt*  
*½ pint milk and water, mixed*

*1 egg yolk and 1 whole egg*  
*1 tablespoon oil*

Beat egg yolk and whole egg together, add the milk and water and the oil. Sift the flour and salt into a bowl, then add the liquid ingredients very slowly and stirring all the time until you have a smooth batter. Allow to rest for at least an hour before using.

For sweet crêpes sift 1 tablespoon of castor sugar with the flour. If liked, 1 tablespoon rum or brandy can be substituted for 1 tablespoon of the milk and water.

Use a small, thick pan for making the pancakes (I use the same pan as I use for omelettes). Melt a little lard or cooking oil in the pan, swirling round to coat the bottom and sides, then pour off any surplus. Pour in a little batter, rotating the pan until there is a thin layer only – too much batter will make a heavy, thick pancake. Cook over moderate heat for about 1 minute until pale golden on the bottom, then toss or turn to other side, using a thin spatula or fish slice if you haven't mastered the art of 'tossing'. Continue until required number of pancakes has been made. They can be stored in refrigerator until required (do not keep longer than 24 hours), then filled just before re-heating and serving.

Make up some Mornay Sauce as directed on page 142. Slice some small mushrooms and cook in a little butter until tender. Chop some cooked chicken into small pieces and mix with mushrooms, then take just enough sauce to bind together. Place a little of this mixture on each pancake, roll up and place side by side in a greased ovenproof dish, in a single layer if possible. Cover with remainder of Mornay sauce and put into a hot oven or under a pre-heated griller until golden brown and heated through. Serve at once.

*Other Fillings:* Follow the directions given above for making the filling, but use any of the following mixtures: chopped chicken and ham; chopped canned asparagus tips with chopped ham; shelled shrimps or chopped prawns and add a little sherry or lemon juice to the sauce; chopped, crisply fried bacon rashers and chopped hard-boiled eggs; or chopped chicken livers sautéed in a little butter before adding to the sauce.

For a delicious accompaniment to grilled or fried chicken

163

fill the pancakes with sweet corn mixed with a little cream, then covered with the Mornay sauce and grilled until golden.

A very quick and simple version is made using canned condensed cream of mushroom soup in place of the Mornay sauce. Add just enough soup to chicken pieces to bind them together, fill pancakes and roll them up, then pour remainder of soup, mixed with a little top milk or cream, over the rolls and grill. Left-over cooked, chopped veal is also good instead of chicken, and asparagus soup can be substituted for the mushroom soup.

## PIZZA

Pizza is an Italian-style pie, made of bread-dough, with a savoury topping, and very useful for many occasions. It can be served for luncheon or even for an informal dinner, made into small individual pizzas or one large one to serve for a buffet supper. The bread dough can be made the night before and quite safely left in the refrigerator until needed, and there is a choice of toppings to suit every taste.

If you have not tried your hand at yeast-dough before you will find this recipe very easy; or if you prefer, the pizza dough can be made with self-raising flour, like a scone dough (page 171).

The yeast dough will keep in the refrigerator for as long as a week, as the action of the yeast in the dough is suspended while in the refrigerator. This same dough can also be used to make a batch of Chelsea buns or some bread rolls, so use half for the pizza and store the other half until next day to make buns or rolls.

When ready to cook the pizza, the dough is lightly rolled out and used to line a pie plate or sandwich tin, topped with desired filling and baked in a moderate oven (350° F or No 4) for 25 to 30 minutes. It should then be served at once.

# BASIC PIZZA DOUGH

| | |
|---|---|
| 1 *lb plain flour* | 2 *teaspoons sugar* |
| 1 *oz yeast* | ½ *teaspoon salt* |
| 2 *oz butter or margarine* | ½ *pint warm milk, or milk and* |
| 2 *eggs* | *water mixed* |
| | *little extra flour* |

These amounts will make two 8-inch pizzas, or use half the dough and store remainder until ready to use for rolls or buns.

Warm the basin in which mixture is made, and sift into it the flour and salt. Cream the yeast and sugar together, then add half the warmed milk, and beaten eggs. Melt butter or margarine in remainder of warm milk. Make a well in middle of flour, pour in the yeast mixture, stirring in lightly, then add the remainder of ingredients, working well together with a wooden spoon, then with your hand. Beat until the mixture begins to leave the bowl and your fingers cleanly (about 5 minutes). Cover with a cloth and put in a warm place to double in size (about 40 minutes). Knead on a lightly floured board, lightly flour the mixing bowl and replace the dough, cover with foil or polythene and put into refrigerator until wanted.

# PIZZA FILLINGS

*Neapolitan Style:* These are made as six 5-inch pizzas.

| | |
|---|---|
| 3 *large, ripe tomatoes* | 1 *clove of garlic* |
| 1 *large onion* | 1 *tablespoon chopped parsley* |
| 1 *small tin anchovy fillets* | *pinch mixed herbs* |
| ¼ *lb salami* | 4 *oz cheese* |
| 2 *tablespoons chopped green olives* | *pizza dough* |

Roll out dough and line 6 greased pie tins, pressing dough in neatly and trimming the edges.

Peel and chop tomatoes, chop anchovies (the oil may be added to the mixture or not as desired), chop salami, finely chop the onion and garlic and coarsely grate the cheese. Mix all ingredients together and divide between the six pie shells. Bake in moderate oven (350° F or No 4) for 20 to 25 minutes until filling is cooked and crust nicely browned. Serve at once.

*Florentine Style:* Lightly roll out half the basic quantities of dough, and line an 8-inch sandwich tin.

| | |
|---|---|
| 4 oz sliced mushrooms | 1 tablespoon chopped green |
| 1 medium onion | pepper |
| 3 oz tomato paste | 4 oz mozzarella cheese |
| 1 rasher bacon | pinch dried oregano or mixed |
| 1½ cups water | herbs |
| | little cooking oil |

Sauté the thinly sliced onion in a little oil until soft, add tomato paste and water and simmer uncovered for 20 minutes until reduced to a smooth sauce. In a separate pan, sauté the mushrooms in a little oil for 5 minutes. Cover the pizza dough with the mushrooms, chopped bacon, green pepper and herbs, then pour tomato-onion sauce over, and top with thinly sliced cheese. Bake in hot oven (400° F or No 6) until crust is nicely browned and filling bubbling and golden. Serve at once.

*Simple Luncheon Pizza:* Shape half the basic dough into a round about ½-inch thick and place on greased baking tin.

| | |
|---|---|
| ¼ lb sliced ham | 1 small can condensed tomato |
| ¼ lb cheese | soup |
| pinch mixed herbs | 1 small can anchovies or sardines |

Cut ham into dice and arrange on top of dough with the drained and chopped anchovies or sardines. Slice the cheese and place over ham mixture, add herbs to tomato soup and pour over top. Bake in a moderate oven (350° F or No 4) until crust is golden brown, about 20 minutes.

Salami can be used instead of ham if desired, and the fish omitted. Chopped stuffed olives or chopped red or green peppers can be added.

## FLAN VARIATIONS

When making pastry you can make up several flan cases and bake them, then allow to cool and store in an airtight tin to serve another day. They will heat up while the filling is cooking.

Or the pastry can be made the night before, rolled out and used to line a flan or sandwich tin, then put into a plastic bag and stored in refrigerator until ready to bake next night.

Excellent short or puff pastry can be bought ready-made and frozen in packets, all ready to be rolled out and used as desired, or you can make up the basic recipe for short pastry and store it covered in the refrigerator for two or three days. This is half as much fat as flour, with $\frac{1}{2}$ teaspoon salt and enough cold water to mix to a stiff dough. Rub the fat into the flour until the mixture is the consistency of breadcrumbs, then with a knife mix in just enough water to make a stiff dough, working quickly until the sides of the bowl are clean. The drier the mixture, the shorter the pastry. Roll out as needed.

To bake blind, line the flan ring or tin with pastry, making a double band round the top and pinching between thumb and finger to make an edging. Cut a piece of greaseproof paper the same size as the bottom of the flan and place over the pastry, then fill with crusts of stale bread or with dried beans or rice. Bake in a moderately hot oven (400° F or No 6) removing the crusts or beans and the paper for the last ten minutes' baking. (The crusts can be rolled out to fine crumbs and stored in a screw-top jar ready for using as a coating when needed.)

With a baked flan case all ready, there are many quickly prepared fillings you can use to make a tasty meal.

*Corn and Bacon Flan:* Remove rind from 4 oz streaky bacon and grill for 2 or 3 minutes on each side. Cut into pieces and place over the bottom of a baked flan case. Beat 2 eggs with salt, pepper and a pinch of dry mustard and add 2 or 3 tablespoons canned sweet corn and ½ cup milk, then pour over the bacon. Bake in moderate oven (375° F or No 5) until mixture is set, about 25 minutes. Serve hot or cold.

*Curried Egg Flan:* Hard-boil 6 eggs, shell and cut into thick slices, and arrange in baked flan case. Make Curry Sauce as directed on page 143, and pour over eggs. Crumble some packaged potato crisps over the top and put into a moderate oven (375° F or No 5) for 10 minutes, until topping is crisped.

*Curried Vegetable Flan:* Extra quantities of vegetables cooked the night before can be made into a tasty flan when covered with Curry Sauce (page 143). Sliced tomatoes can be added to cooked peas, beans, carrots, or cauliflower for the filling, then covered with the curry sauce and baked for 10 minutes.

# Quick Dishes from the Kitchen Cupboard

The businesswoman-housewife needs to keep a well-stocked cupboard in the kitchen for those times when there are unexpected guests for meals, or those occasions when she has been kept working so late that the shops are closed and there is nothing prepared for dinner.

There are so many good foods obtainable today in cans, packets, bottles, frozen or dehydrated, that almost any kind of meal can be prepared in quick time. And all these ingredients are here to stay – they are accepted by the young women of today, so that many of our old and tried recipes have become redundant, superseded by the can-opener.

But there is still room for new recipes using the whole range of prepared foods, and you can make up a good dinner which demonstrates that some thought and attention have gone into its preparation, even if it is only combining a can of salmon, a packet of ready-mixed sauce and a pastry flan which you baked a few days ago and stored in a tin. Garnish it with canned mushrooms and strips of canned pimento and you have a dish which will taste as good as it looks.

Keep a supply of canned condensed soups, and you will always have ready a quick asparagus sauce for chicken, or mushroom sauce to serve with frozen fish fingers to give them new flavour.

Make Creole eggs for breakfast, lunch or dinner simply by breaking eggs into individual ovenproof ramekins, then adding a tablespoon of tomato soup, straight from the can, over the eggs. Sprinkle with packaged grated cheese and bake until set.

F*

Chicken and beef bouillon cubes are invaluable for making stock, sauces or soup, and have the added advantage of not taking up much room in the cupboard.

A can of macaroni cheese will satisfy three hungry people if you add two rashers of bacon which have been fried and crumbled into the macaroni along with a chopped onion, also fried in the bacon fat. Turn this mixture into a casserole, sprinkle the top with grated cheese and bake until it is bubbling hot. Or chop up some peeled tomatoes, or canned mushrooms and add to the macaroni casserole.

A can of potato salad looks and tastes better with the addition of chopped parsley, grated raw carrot and a little chopped or sliced canned pimento. Or add chopped anchovies and chopped chives and serve in lettuce cups as the first course for dinner, garnished with sliced tomatoes.

You need never despair of a sweet finish to a meal with a can of creamed rice which can be divided between four sweet dishes, topped with a canned peach and a grating of block chocolate. Or turn a well-drained can of apricots into a baked pastry case, beat two egg whites with a tablespoon of sugar and a pinch of mixed spice, and spread it over the top of the apricots. Put into a hot oven just long enough to turn golden, and there is a party dessert.

Never despise the power of a can-opener in an emergency.

## READY-BLEND FLOUR MIX

This flour mix is suitable for a wide variety of recipes such as cakes, scones, tea cakes, or instead of pastry. Make it in the quantities given here, store in an airtight container, and it will keep in the refrigerator for up to two months. Be sure to label the container and mark it with the date of making.

3 *lb self-raising flour*          1 *lb margarine*
3 *teaspoons salt*

Sift flour and salt twice into a bowl. Rub in the fat until mixture is like fine crumbs. Store in jars or well-sealed polythene bags, and use as required.

## QUICK HERB SCONES OR DUMPLINGS

12 oz mix                                    ¼ pint milk
1 teaspoon dried mixed herbs, or
    fresh herbs to taste

Mix to a soft dough with the milk and press out about ¾-inch thick on a lightly floured board. Cut into rounds or wedges, brush over with milk and place on a floured baking sheet. Bake in a hot oven (450° F or No 8) for 15 to 20 minutes, or place on top of simmering stew, cover and continue cooking for 25 to 30 minutes. If placed on top of casserole in the oven, continue baking, with the heat turned up if possible, but do not replace lid.

Sweet scones or a topping for stewed apples or other fruit can be made in the same way, replacing herbs with sugar and ground cinnamon or mixed spice to taste. Chopped dates or seeded raisins could also be added to the mixture.

## SWEET AND SOUR PORK

This is a quick version of a popular Chinese dish, which you can make using a large can of pork luncheon meat from your emergency cupboard, and serving it with a simple sweet-sour sauce. The meat is cut into cubes (any excess fat being removed), then dipped into batter and fried in deep hot fat or oil until crisp and golden brown. Make the sauce and pour over the meat, then serve with rice.

**FOR THE BATTER**

4 *oz self-raising flour*                    *salt and pepper*
¼ *pint milk (or half milk and*
  *half water)*

**FOR THE SAUCE**

1 *medium onion, sliced thin*        ½ *cup vinegar*
1 *small carrot, grated coarsely*    1 *tablespoon sugar*
1 *stalk of celery or ½ green pepper,*   1 *cup stock (made with a bouillon*
  *sliced thin*                          *cube)*
1 *level tablespoon cornflour*

Blend the milk into the sifted dry ingredients to make a smooth batter. Dip cubed meat into this, coating well, then fry until golden. Drain on kitchen paper and keep hot while the sauce cooks.

Add prepared vegetables to hot stock and cook for 5 minutes. Blend cornflour with vinegar and stir into vegetables, stirring until thickened. Add sugar and stir until dissolved. Pour over fried meat cubes, arranged on a bed of rice.

## HONEY-GLAZED HAM

Cooked, canned hams are very useful for either hot or cold meals, and this way of re-heating the ham makes it into a special meal.

Remove ham from tin and scrape off all the jelly around it. but do not discard this. When ham is quite tidy, brush over with slightly warmed honey, then sprinkle with fine browned breadcrumbs, pressing the breadcrumbs into the honey. Mix ¼ pint pineapple juice and ¼ pint vinegar together. Place ham on an ovenproof dish which can be brought to the table for serving. Pour the vinegar-pineapple mixture over the ham and bake in a hot oven (425° F or No 7) for 20 to 30 minutes, basting occasionally, until ham is nicely browned. The jelly scraped from the ham can be put round it in the dish to melt and blend with the basting juices.

Pineapple slices can be browned in butter and used to garnish the ham, and if tomatoes are available, cut in halves and bake round the ham, serving each tomato on a slice of pineapple.

# Puddings and Desserts
### INCLUDING ICE CREAMS

The majority of the recipes given in this chapter are for special desserts for a dinner party.

For the family there are a number of recipes which can be made up in quick time on returning home, and the children will always be happy with a dish of ice cream and fruit, or a quickly made sundae. During the winter, if you have a ready baked pie shell or flan case on hand, it is very easy to fill it with fruit and re-heat in a few minutes, or even with a custard or chocolate pudding made from flavoured cornflour and milk.

Keep a good stock of canned fruits, a few packets of chocolate or caramel flavoured cornflour, packets of seeded raisins or sultanas, a few tins of creamed rice pudding and some cans of cream, and you are never at a loss to provide a sweet ending to a meal in a matter of minutes.

## ORANGE TOAST SLICES

A recipe for the family. These slices make a delicious pudding to serve for supper on a cold night.

| | |
|---|---|
| 6 *slices stale bread, cut ¾-inch thick* | ⅓ *cup orange juice* |
| 1 *egg* | 2 *teaspoons sugar* |
| 1 *teaspoon grated orange rind* | *butter or vegetable oil* |
| ¼ *teaspoon cinnamon* | *honey* |

Remove crusts from bread slices. Beat egg with sugar until

frothy, then add cinnamon, orange juice and rind and beat again to blend well. Dip slices of bread in the egg-orange mixture. Have the butter or oil hot in a large frying pan and fry the bread slices, two at a time, until golden brown and crisp, turning to brown both sides. Remove from pan and drain on paper. Repeat with other slices, adding more oil if necessary. Serve slices hot with a spoonful of slightly warmed honey on each.

The slices can also be served with hot custard sauce or with cream if desired.


## DESSERT OMELETTES

Follow directions for making soufflé omelettes as given on page 160. Prepare the filling before making up the omelette and be ready to take it straight to the table to serve as it comes from the pan. Instead of salt and pepper in recipe, any desired flavouring can be added.

Grated chocolate can be added to the beaten egg whites before folding into the yolks, or 1 teaspoon instant coffee can be blended with the milk to give a mocha flavour.

Put well drained canned peaches or apricots through an electric blender, or mash with a fork until smooth. Add 2 tablespoons syrup drained from fruit and a little sherry or a few drops of lemon juice. Heat, but do not allow to boil, stir in 1 teaspoon butter and serve as a filling for omelettes.

A tasty trick for omelettes is to make up a quantity of brandy or rum butter, freeze it until hard, then place a small square of the butter on each omelette before folding over. Try adding ½ teaspoon ground mixed spice to the omelette mixture before cooking.

Make the flavoured butter by blending together 4 oz each of butter and castor sugar. Add 2 oz ground almonds and 1 or 2 tablespoons of brandy or rum, blend well and form into a square. Put into 'fridge to set, then cut into small squares or slices.

## CHOCOLATE ROYALE MERINGUE

This is one of the most fabulous desserts I have ever tasted, and is well worth all the effort you put into making it. It has a meringue base lined with crunchy chocolate, and then filled with a luscious creamy chocolate mixture, finished off with whipped cream. As you can see, it is very rich and serves should not be too generous, so the amounts given here will make a very special dessert for 8 or 10 people. It should be made the night before serving and chilled in refrigerator.

**FOR MERINGUE SHELL**

| | |
|---|---|
| 4 *egg whites* | 1 *teaspoon vinegar* |
| 4 *oz castor sugar* | 1 *teaspoon ground cinnamon* |
| 4 *oz granulated sugar* | *pinch salt* |

**FOR THE CHOCOLATE FILLING**

| | |
|---|---|
| 6 *oz semi-sweet chocolate* | ½ *cup water* |
| 4 *egg yolks* | |

**FOR CREAM FILLING**

| | |
|---|---|
| ½ *pint whipping cream* | *scant ½ teaspoon ground cinnamon* |
| 1 *dessertspoon castor sugar* | *chopped walnuts* |

Draw an 8-inch circle on a piece of thick white paper and brush over well with vegetable oil. Place paper on oven tray.

Make the meringue by adding salt to egg whites and beating until stiff. Gradually beat in half the sugar, a spoonful at a time, then fold in remainder of sugar, adding the vinegar and cinnamon. Spread this meringue within the circle drawn on the paper, hollowing out the middle but leaving a layer on the bottom about ¼-inch thick. The sides should be about

2 inches high, and smooth on the outside. Bake in a slow oven (250° F or No ½) for about 1¼ hours, or until meringue is set. Remove from oven and allow to cool, very carefully peeling away the paper and placing the meringue case on a plate which can be brought to the table for serving.

Melt the chocolate in a basin over hot water. Cool slightly and spoon 3 tablespoons of the liquid chocolate over the inside of the cooled meringue case. Add the lightly beaten egg yolks and water to remainder of melted chocolate, and cook in a double saucepan over hot water until the custard thickens. Combine the cream, sugar and cinnamon and whip until thick. Spread a layer of cream over the cooled, set chocolate layer in the meringue, then fold remainder of cream into chocolate custard and fill into meringue. Chill overnight.

When ready to serve swirl top with a little more whipped cream if desired, and sprinkle with chopped nuts, or if preferred garnish top of chocolate mixture with chopped walnuts.

## MERINGUE TORTE

Another delicious dessert using meringue as the base for a luscious filling, but this one is made in layers with a creamy filling, and chilled overnight, ready to come straight to the table.

Make up the meringue as directed in Chocolate Royale Meringue, but omit the cinnamon. Divide the meringue mixture between two 8-inch sandwich tins with removable bases, placing an oiled round of paper in each tin. Smooth tops of meringue and bake in a slow oven (250° F or No ½) for about 1½ hours, or until meringue is quite firm. Do not allow to colour too much. Cool in the tins, then carefully remove and peel off the paper. Place one meringue on plate in which torte is to be served.

FILLING

½ *pint double cream*
½ *cup seeded raisins*
½ *cup maraschino cherries*
*few pieces crystallized ginger, if*
   *liked*

1 *tablespoon brandy or sherry*
*chopped walnuts*

Pour boiling water over raisins and leave for 10 minutes to swell. Drain well and chop small. Drain cherries and chop small, and chop the ginger very finely, removing as much sugar as possible from the ginger. Put into a basin with raisins and cherries and add brandy or sherry, mixing well. Stand for ½ an hour, stirring occasionally, then drain fruit well and fold into stiffly whipped cream. Spread ⅓ of cream over meringue layer on plate, cover with other meringue layer, and spread remainder of cream over top and sides of torte. Sprinkle top with nuts.


## PEACH MERINGUE PIE

If the preceding recipe is rather rich for you, try this one with its filling of peaches and cream. Make a meringue shell as directed in above recipe, but instead of adding cinnamon to the meringue, fold in 2 oz finely chopped blanched almonds.

When meringue is baked and cooled put aside in a cool, dry place until just before serving time. Whip ½ pint double cream until thick, add a few drops of almond essence and 1 teaspoon sugar. Drain a small can of sliced peaches. Put half the whipped cream in the meringue case, add sliced chpeaes and cover with remainder of cream. Decorate with glacé cherries and serve at once.

For a change, substitute strawberry ice cream for the cearm, or when fresh strawberries are available, use them instead of sliced peaches.

# GRAPEFRUIT SUPREME

This is an unusual way of serving grapefruit as a dessert, and one which would add sweet interest to any dinner party. The fruit is prepared in the morning before leaving home, and a meringue topping is baked on top about 15 minutes before serving.

| | |
|---|---|
| 3 *large or* 6 *small grapefruit* | 3 *egg whites* |
| 1 *apple* | 6 *oz castor sugar* |
| 2 *bananas* | *pinch salt* |
| 1 *large orange* | 1 *tablespoon cherry brandy* |
| *cherries, either fresh or bottled* | *extra sugar if needed* |

These are cooked in 6 ovenproof ramekins in which they are also brought to the table to serve.

In the morning cut grapefruit in halves if using large ones, or cut a slice from the tops of the small ones. Using a curved grapefruit knife, cut round the skins to remove pulp. Cut away any white pith and tough membranes and chop the pulp. Put into a basin with peeled, cored and chopped apple, sliced bananas, peeled and chopped orange and chopped cherries. Add cherry brandy and sugar if necessary, but remember meringue topping will add sweetness. Put fruit into refrigerator to chill until ready to serve. Wrap grapefruit shells in a plastic bag and also store in refrigerator until needed.

Just before serving time place the grapefruit shells in the ramekins and spoon in the fruit, draining away excess juice (which can be used for a sauce or jellied sweet next day). Whip the egg whites with the salt until stiff, then gradually beat in the sugar, beating until sugar is dissolved and meringue is stiff. Pile the meringue on top of each filled grapefruit, taking it down to the edge of the grapefruit shell, and forming into peaks with a fork. Sprinkle top of each one with a very little sugar and put into a fairly slow oven (300° F or No 1) until meringue is set and pale golden on top. Serve at once. For 6.


# MOCHA-ALMOND MOUSSE

A mousse is a deliciously light dessert which is much easier to make than it looks, but it is not everyday fare, so reserve this recipe (and the one following) for festive occasions. The mousse is made up the night before, but it should not be served too cold, so remove from refrigerator at least half an hour before serving. The mixture can be set in a mould and turned out to serve, or it can be made in a serving dish which can be brought to the table. The same mixture can also be divided between 6 small individual moulds if liked, and turned out to serve.

1 *oz cornflour*
½ *pint milk*
2 *oz plain chocolate, grated*
½ *pint strong coffee*
*pinch salt*

2 *oz castor sugar*
1 *whole egg and* 1 *extra yolk*
½ *oz gelatine*
1 *tablespoon thick cream*
*slivered, blanched almonds*
*whipped cream*

Blend cornflour to a smooth paste with a little milk. Put remainder of milk on to boil, add grated chocolate, and stir until dissolved. When boiling, pour milk over blended cornflour, return to pan, add coffee and stir until boiling again. Add sugar and cool slightly, then add beaten egg yolks and mix well. Dissolve gelatine in 1 tablespoon hot water and add to chocolate mixture. Cool. Beat egg white until stiff and fold into mixture, then whip cream and fold in also. Pour into wetted mould and leave to set. Turn out before serving and sprinkle with slivered almonds. Serve with whipped cream.

# LEMON MOUSSE

This is a good recipe to make up after you have been making meringues (page 176), as it helps use up the egg yolks. But that is not its only recommendation, as you will find it a delicious dessert. When strawberries are available, use them to garnish the mousse after turning out of its mould, or pineapple chunks are also good with the lemon flavouring of the mousse.

| | |
|---|---|
| 1 *large lemon* | 2 *egg yolks* |
| ½ *pint milk* | ½ *oz gelatine* |
| 1 *dessertspoon cornflour* | 2 *tablespoons thick cream* |
| 2 *oz castor sugar* | *fruit to garnish* |
| | *whipped cream* |

Wash lemon and carefully peel off the yellow part of the rind. Warm the milk and infuse lemon rind in it for 15 minutes. Remove rind and bring milk to boil, then stir in cornflour which has been blended to a paste with a little milk, and continue stirring until boiling. Add sugar, then cool slightly. Squeeze juice from lemon and measure, making up to ½ pint with hot water, and dissolve gelatine in it. Beat egg yolks into cornflour mixture, and when quite cool, strain dissolved gelatine into custard, whisking well. When mixture starts to thicken, fold in the 2 tablespoons cream which has been lightly whipped, and pour mousse into a wetted mould. Turn out when ready to serve and garnish with fruit and whipped cream.

# PASTRY FLAN CASE

If you have several baked flan cases ready made and stored in an airtight tin, you can always serve a dessert in a hurry.

These cases can be filled with fruit and glazed, or with a custard filling and served hot, after crisping the flan case in the oven for a few minutes. See page 184 for suggestions for fillings.

You can use bought pastry, some of the quick-blend flour mix (page 170), or make up a rich shortcrust pastry given here, just as time dictates.

| | |
|---|---|
| 8 *oz plain flour* | 2 *tablespoons castor sugar* |
| 1 *teaspoon salt* | 1 *egg yolk* |
| 5 *oz butter, or a mixture of butter* | *cold water* |
| *and margarine* | |

Sieve flour and salt into basin. Rub in fat with tips of fingers until like fine breadcrumbs. Add sugar. Beat egg yolk with 1 tablespoon cold water and add just enough to make a firm dough. Turn out on a lightly floured board, knead or pat gently into a round, then roll out into a round $\frac{1}{4}$-inch thick and about 1 inch larger all round than the flan ring or pie plate. Press into position, being careful not to stretch pastry. Trim edges with a sharp knife, and if using pie plate, put a $\frac{1}{2}$-inch border of pastry all round edge, and crimp edges together. Prick bottom lightly with a fork. Chill for half an hour before baking.

If the pastry case is to be baked 'blind', that is without a filling, cut a piece of greased paper just the size of the case and put on the bottom, greased side down, then half fill with rice or dried beans to keep the bottom of the case flat.

Bake in a hot oven (450° F or No 8) for about 15 minutes, until pastry is almost cooked and edges are golden. Remove filling and paper and return case to oven for a few minutes to dry off and finish cooking. Remove the flan ring and place on rack to cool. Do not keep longer than 3 or 4 days in a tin.

# NO-BAKE PIE SHELLS

As a change from the usual baked pastry case, make one of these no-bake cases with either cereal or biscuit crumbs. They are best made the night before and left to chill overnight, then filled in the morning before leaving home. A variety of fillings can be used, several of which are given on the following pages. Gingernut or arrowroot biscuits can be used if preferred.

*6 oz wholemeal biscuits*       *½ cup melted butter or margarine*
*⅓ cup sugar*

Crush biscuits to fine crumbs, either by putting through the fine blade of a mincing machine, or crushing with a rolling pin. Blend well with sugar and melted butter, then press firmly into a lightly greased pie plate, smoothing down evenly over base and sides. Leave overnight to set, and fill next morning.

*6 oz cornflakes*       *2 oz butter or margarine*
*2 oz sugar*

Follow above directions, but if you want to make this in the morning, put into a moderate oven for 10 minutes to crisp. Fill when you return home and serve at once.

# LEMON AND HONEY CRUNCH PIE

Instead of a pastry base, this pie has a crunchy crust made of crushed biscuits. The whole pie is prepared the night before and stored in refrigerator until half an hour before serving. It is then removed and decorated with swirls of whipped cream.

CRUNCH CRUST

2 *cups crushed biscuit crumbs*          $\frac{1}{3}$ *cup melted butter*
1 *or 2 tablespoons honey*

FILLING

2 *eggs*                                  *grated rind 1 lemon*
1 *tablespoon honey*                      $\frac{1}{4}$ *cup evaporated milk, chilled*
$\frac{1}{2}$ *pint milk*                 *whipped cream*
$\frac{1}{4}$ *cup strained lemon juice*

Crush the biscuits between two sheets of white paper, using a rolling pin. Put honey and butter in a bowl and stand over hot water until slightly melted, then mix with crumbs. Press this mixture evenly over the base and sides of a lightly buttered 8-inch pie plate. Chill until firm. The amount of honey needed depends on the kind of biscuits used, Milk Arrowroot being good for this crust.

FILLING

Slightly warm the honey and add to the beaten egg yolks. Heat milk and stir into egg yolks, then place in top half of a double boiler over hot water and stir over heat until mixture coats the back of a spoon. Remove from heat, add lemon rind and juice, and allow to cool. When cold, fold in stiffly beaten egg whites and the whipped evaporated milk. Turn into the crunch crust and chill until set. Before serving, whip the cream and swirl round the edge of the pie. To serve 6.

# FILLINGS FOR FLANS OR PIE-SHELLS

*Rice-Meringue Pie:* Turn a can of creamed rice into the prepared flan or pie shell. Soak some seeded raisins or sultanas in hot water for a few minutes, then drain well and dry. Scatter over the top of the rice. Beat 1 or 2 egg whites until stiff, then beat in 1 dessertspoon sugar and spread meringue over the top of the rice mixture, taking it right to the edges of the pastry. Bake in a slow oven for 25 to 30 minutes, until the meringue is set and golden on top. Serve at once.

*Jellied Fruit Flan :* Drain syrup from a small can of sliced peaches (or any other fruit preferred), and measure ¼ pint of juice into a small saucepan. Add 2 teaspoons powdered gelatine and stir over gentle heat until dissolved. Cool. Arrange sliced peaches in the prepared flan or pie shell in a regular pattern. When jelly is just beginning to set, spoon over fruit. Put aside in a cool place until set. Serve with cream or chilled custard.

*Ice Cream Pie :* Fill one of the no-bake pie shells (page 183) with spoonfuls of alternate vanilla and chocolate ice cream. Sprinkle grated chocolate over the top and serve at once.

*Glazed Fruit Flan :* Drain 1 small can pear halves and 1 small can cherries. Arrange sliced pears and cherries in a pattern in baked flan case. Measure ¼ pint fruit syrup. Blend 2 teaspoons arrowroot with a little of the syrup, and put remainder of fruit syrup into a small saucepan with 1 tablespoon redcurrant jelly, and bring to boil. Stir in blended arrowroot, and continue stirring until mixture is quite clear and thickening. Pour over fruit in flan case, filling it to the top. Put aside to cool and set. Serve with cream or chilled custard.

*Apple Jelly Flan :* Instead of pears and cherries, as in above recipe, use sliced apples which have been cooked until tender (but not broken) in a little water and lemon juice. Drain carefully, and use juice to make glaze as directed above.

*Apple Meringue Flan :* Fill baked flan case with cooked apples which have been sweetened and beaten with a fork until smooth. Prepare meringue as in Rice-Meringue Pie (page 184), spread over the apples and bake until meringue is set and golden. Serve at once.

## FLAMING CHERRIES

A wonderful finish to a good dinner, especially on a cold night when the table is lighted only by candles. The idea of this dessert is to make a spectacular entrance carrying the flaming cherries, and allow the guests to help themselves, spooning the cherries over dishes of ice cream. No preparations beforehand are needed for this dish, unless you prefer to make your own ice cream the night before.

| | |
|---|---|
| 2 *lb can of black cherries* | *large block vanilla ice cream* |
| ½ *lb blackcurrant jelly* | *wineglass of brandy* |

Drain juice from cherries, and place them in an ovenproof dish which can be brought to the table for serving. Spread the jelly in a layer over the cherries and put into a moderately hot oven for 10 to 15 minutes, until heated through. Divide the ice cream between 6 individual sweet dishes, leaving plenty of room on top for the cherries to be added. When ready to serve, remove cherries from oven and pour the slightly warmed brandy over the top. Set it alight and carry flaming cherries to the table for guests to help themselves.

## MIXED FRUIT GATEAU

This is a dessert which is best made in the morning before leaving home, and it does not take very long to assemble if you leave all the ingredients ready the night before. In the evening it only needs to be covered with whipped cream before serving. The sponge cake can either be made the night before or you can buy good sponges from your local cake shop.

| | |
|---|---|
| 2-*layer sponge cake* | 1 *pint whipping cream* |
| 1 *small can sliced peaches* | ½ *cup sherry or port wine* |
| 1 *small can apricots* | *maraschino cherries* |
| 1 *cup strawberry jam* | |

Cut each sponge layer in halves through the middle to make 4 layers. Drain the fruit (keep the juice to make a jelly next day), and chop pieces fairly small but put aside 6 peach slices. Whip half the cream until thick. Put a layer of cake on a plate suitable for bringing to the table, and spread with a layer of strawberry jam, then with chopped apricots and a thin layer of cream. Repeat this with other two cake layers, using chopped peaches for middle layer. Cover with a sponge layer, and sprinkle sherry or wine over the top. Stand in a cool place until just before serving. Whip remaining cream and cover layer cake completely on top and sides with cream. Decorate top with sliced peaches and well drained cherries. Cut in wedges to serve. This gives 8 good serves.

## CHOCOLATE-GINGER PUDDING

Use packaged chocolate pudding powder to make this simple pudding, which is especially popular with the children. Make up the night before and chill until ready to serve.

| | |
|---|---|
| 1 *packet chocolate pudding powder* | 1 *tablespoon sugar* |
| ¾ *pint milk* | *gingernut biscuits* |
| ½ *teaspoon mixed spice* | *cream* |

Make up chocolate pudding with milk as directed on packet, adding mixed spice and sugar. Grease a square loaf tin and line bottom and sides with gingernut biscuits. Put half chocolate pudding into prepared tin, add another layer of gingernuts and then remainder of pudding. Chill overnight.

When ready to serve, run a knife round the sides of the tin to loosen pudding, then turn out on a serving dish. Serve with cream if desired.


# VIENNA CHEESECAKE

A well-made cheesecake is one of the most delicious desserts you can serve as the finale to a good dinner, and this is a very acceptable version of a recipe which is made in many different countries. It should be made the night before serving, and when cold, wrapped lightly in foil and stored in the refrigerator. Remove at least half an hour before serving to take away the chilled flavour. These amounts will serve 6.

**PASTRY**

6 *oz plain flour*
*pinch salt*
3 *oz butter or margarine*

1 *teaspoon castor sugar*
1 *egg yolk*
*little water if necessary*

**FILLING**

2 *oz butter or margarine*
3 *oz castor sugar*
2 *eggs*
1½ *oz ground almonds*

8 *oz cottage cheese*
1 *oz semolina*
2 *oz seeded raisins*
*grated rind and juice* 1 *lemon*

Make pastry by sifting flour and salt into a basin. Rub in the fat until mixture resembles coarse breadcrumbs, stir in sugar. Mix to a firm paste with beaten egg yolk, adding a little water if necessary for right consistency. Roll out on a lightly floured board. Stand an 8-inch flan ring on a baking tray and line with pastry, pressing down well. Trim edges.

To make the filling, cream the sugar and butter together

until light and fluffy. Separate yolks and whites of eggs, and beat the yolks into the ground almonds and semolina, then beat in cottage cheese, chopped raisins, lemon juice and grated rind. Fold this mixture into the creamed mixture as lightly as possible, but blend ingredients well together. Whisk the egg whites until stiff and fold into mixture. Turn into the pastry-lined flan ring and bake in a moderate oven (350° F or No 4) for 50 to 55 minutes until pastry is golden and filling firm. Stand for a few minutes, then lift off flan ring, and allow to cool before storing in refrigerator.


## GOLDEN GLAZED PEARS

When you want to serve a hot dessert, but don't feel like a substantial pudding, make these golden glazed pears, which can be served with a hot custard sauce or with cream. Cooking time about 15 minutes.

| | |
|---|---|
| 1 *large can pear halves* | 6 *oz sweet orange marmalade* |
| 1 *teaspoon butter* | *cream or custard* |

Open the can of pears and turn into a saucepan to heat without boiling. When pear halves are hot, lift out with a slotted spoon and keep hot on a dish over boiling water. Measure ½ pint pear syrup back onto saucepan and cook quickly over high heat to reduce for about 5 minutes. Stir in marmalade and heat again. The marmalade mixture should have the consistency of a thick sauce. Remove from heat and stir in butter until completely melted, then pour over pear halves. Serve at once.

As a change, redcurrant jelly can be used instead of marmalade, but if mixture is too sweet it may be necessary to add a few drops of lemon juice. For a special dessert, a little red wine could be added when using redcurrant jelly.

# PINEAPPLE JELLY ROLL

This makes an attractive looking dessert which is very easy to make the night before serving. It is turned out and coated with either whipped cream or cottage cheese just before the meal, then cut into slices at the table. These amounts will give 6 good serves.

| | |
|---|---|
| 1 *large can of pineapple slices* | 1 *lb cottage cheese* or ½ *pint* |
| 1 *packet lime-flavoured jelly* | *whipping cream* |
| 1 *tablespoon lemon juice or sherry* | *preserved cherries* |

Open can carefully to get a smooth edge, drain out the juice into a measuring jug, and put well-drained pineapple slices back into can. Add lemon juice or sherry to juice and if necessary bring amount of liquid up to ¾ pint with water. Heat liquid without allowing to boil and stir in jelly tablets, continuing to stir until completely dissolved. Cool slightly, then pour into can with pineapple slices, filling as full as possible. Chill overnight. If there is any jelly over, pour it into a flat dish to set.

When ready to serve, open can from other end and push jelly roll out on to serving dish. Stick a row of wooden cocktail sticks into the pineapple slices to act as a guide for cutting. Coat the slice all over with whipped cream or smoothly beaten cottage cheese (sweeten to taste if necessary) and place a row of cherries to mark the slices, removing the cocktail sticks.

# STRAWBERRIES JAMAICA

When strawberries are in season, make the most of them with easily prepared desserts such as this one and those that follow. All can be prepared ahead of serving time, either the night before or in the morning. But remember to remove

...ey are combined with orange juice and rind to make
...licious dessert, which is made the night before serving.
...ly needs to be coated with whipped cream before servin

| | |
|---|---|
| ...*lb cooking apples* | *6 oz soft white breadcrumbs* |
| ...*ice 1 orange* | *4 oz butter or margarine* |
| ...*rated rind of 1 orange* | *6 oz Demerara sugar* |
| ...*tablespoon sugar* | *¼ pint double cream for whippi* |
| ...*or 3 whole cloves* | |

...eel, core and slice apples and cook with 1 tablespoon suga
...whole cloves, and just enough orange juice to prevent appl
...urning. When soft, beat apples with a fork to make a smoot
...urée. Remove cloves. Melt butter or margarine in a larg
...frying pan and fry the breadcrumbs slowly, stirring all th
...time to brown evenly, but do not let them become too dark
...Turn crumbs into a bowl and add half orange rind an
...Demerara sugar, mixing well together.

...Grease a 7-inch flan ring and put in centre of a flat plate
...Put ⅓ of crumb mixture in the flan ring, cover with half the
...apple purée, then repeat these layers, finishing with a layer
...of crumb mixture. Pat down firmly, and store in refrigerator.
...When ready to serve next day whip the cream lightly.
...Remove flan ring, and coat pudding with cream. Sprinkle
...with remaining orange rind and serve at once.

## ALMOND FRITTERS

An ideal family dessert which can be prepared and cooked
in about 20 minutes, then served at once.

| | |
|---|---|
| 2 *eggs, separated* | *few drops vanilla essence* |
| 1 *oz castor sugar* | *oil for frying* |
| 2 *oz ground almonds* | *extra sugar* |
| ½ *oz cornflour* | *lemon wedges for garnish* |

from refrigerator a little time before serving, as extreme cold
takes away some of the flavour.

Mix equal quantities of fresh, hulled strawberries and
pineapple cubes (either fresh or canned). Add sugar to taste,
a tablespoon pineapple juice and a tablespoon rum, and toss
lightly to mix well. Store in refrigerator. Serve with lightly
whipped cream.

Another version of this dessert is to use raspberries and
pineapple together, and substitute brandy or kirsch for the rum.

If making the dessert for children, use more pineapple
juice and omit the alcohol.

## STRAWBERRY LAYER PIE

First make an 8-inch pastry case and bake it blind (see
page 167). That is done the night before, and the pie is filled
just before serving. If you make your own ice cream, that
also can be made the night before, otherwise bring home a
family block, using either strawberry or vanilla.

| | |
|---|---|
| 2 *cups halved strawberries* | *6 or 8 whole berries to garnish* |
| 2 *tablespoons redcurrant jelly* | *ice cream* |
| *pastry case* | |

Take 1 cup strawberries and mix them with 1 tablespoon redcurrant jelly, then spread this over the base of the pastry
case. Spoon half the ice cream over this layer, then repeat
with remainder of strawberries and jelly, and finish with a
layer of ice cream. Decorate with whole strawberries, and
chill until you are ready to serve, but don't allow the ice
cream to melt before serving or the effect of the red and white
layers is spoilt.

If you have a home-freezer, this pie could be made up at
any time when strawberries are in season, then frozen. It
should be allowed to thaw out completely before serving.

# STRAWBERRY WHIP

This is a recipe which you can prepare just before serving, but the strawberries should be left ready to be added to the mixture. Either sweet sherry or cherry brandy is good for this, or if preferred use a little orange or lemon juice.

1 *cup hulled and chopped straw-*       pinch salt
     *berries*      ¼ *cup castor sugar*
1 *dessertspoon sweet sherry*      ½ *pint whipping cream*
2 *egg whites*      4 *whole strawberries*

Chop the strawberries in the morning and add sherry, then put into refrigerator to chill until ready to make the whip. Beat egg whites with the salt until stiff, then beat in sugar gradually until meringue is stiff and glossy. Whip the cream and fold into meringue, then lastly fold in strawberries. Divide between four sweet dishes and top each with a whole strawberry. Serve at once.

# STRAWBERRIES MARIE-THERESE

Simplicity itself, but there are few desserts which are more delicious than this one, either for a party or a family dinner. The amounts given here will give 6 generous serves. Prepare the fruit overnight, or in the morning before leaving home, then store in refrigerator. Remove at least 20 minutes before serving, as the fruit lose some of their flavour if served too cold.

1 *lb fresh, ripe strawberries*      1 *tablespoon orange juice*
1 *lb ripe redcurrants*      ½ *cup sweet white wine*
1 *lb ripe raspberries*      *whipping cream*
*sugar to taste*      1 *teaspoon castor sugar*

Wash, drain and hull berries and mix together in a bowl.

Sprinkle with sugar and add orange juice an[...] refrigerator until ready to serve.

Remove fruit, and stand at room temper[...] 20 minutes. Divide between 6 sweet dishes (it [...] attractive in glass dishes), and top with the c[...] been lightly whipped with the castor sugar.

# STRAWBERRY BAKED AL[...]

This is a most spectacular dessert for special occ[...] preparations can be done beforehand, but[...] assembled and baked for 10 minutes at the ver[...] Either fresh or frozen strawberries can be used[...]

*single layer sponge cake*      *meringue (as gi[...]*
1 *lb strawberries*      176)
1 *large block of vanilla ice cream*

Pick over and hull the strawberries, using only [...] berries. Arrange them on top of sponge cake, leav[...] border of cake all round. Cover strawberries wi[...] of ice cream, being careful to leave the border [...] into freezing part of refrigerator while you mak[...] Cover the whole cake with the meringue, and pla[...] thick ovenproof plate. Make sure the meringue c[...] bit of the ice cream, and seal it to the edge of the[...]

Have the oven very hot (500° F) and put the A[...] cold oven slide in the middle of the oven for just lo[...] to set the meringue and tint it pale golden. Rer[...] oven and serve it at once, cut in wedges.

# APPLE AND ORANGE CAK[...]

There are very few people who do not like apples,[...]

Beat egg yolks and sugar together until creamy. Beat in ground almonds, cornflour and vanilla. Beat egg whites until stiff and fold into almond mixture. Have a deep saucepan of oil hot enough lightly to brown a cube of bread dropped into the oil, but do not allow it to smoke. Drop spoonfuls of the mixture into the hot fat and fry until golden and puffed. Drain on paper and serve at once, lightly sprinkled with sugar, and garnished with lemon quarters.

## ICE CREAM DESSERTS

If your refrigerator has a large frozen-food compartment there are an almost endless variety of frozen desserts you can make with ice cream. With a tray of ice cream ready made in the refrigerator you need never be at a loss for either family or dinner-party sweets, even if you have only a few minutes to prepare them.

For special occasions make up two or three different ice-bombes or ice cream cakes, and freeze them ready to serve when required. They should keep in the frozen-food compartment for several weeks, but if they have once thawed do not attempt to re-freeze. Either home-made or bought ice cream can be used for these, and although quite simple to make, an iced bombe always looks very special when you entertain friends for dinner.

I use an aluminium pudding basin to make bombes, but if you have any fancy moulds they look rather attractive when the iced mixture is turned out, and they can be garnished with fresh berries, grated chocolate, slivered toasted almonds, chopped cherries or just served plain as desired.

## CREAMY ICE CREAM (1)

This is the simplest way of making ice cream, especially for the busy woman, as it can be made and left in the refrigerator without needing to be beaten again during freezing time.

2 *egg whites*  
*pinch salt*  
½ *pint whipping cream*

2 *tablespoons icing sugar*  
½ *teaspoon vanilla*

Beat the egg whites with salt until stiff enough to stand in peaks. Whip cream until slightly thickened, fold in icing sugar and vanilla, then fold in egg whites, blending all together lightly. Turn into freezing trays and freeze until firm.

## CREAMY ICE CREAM (2)

Another way of making ice cream is to make a boiled custard with 2 eggs and ½ pint milk, and when cold fold in ½ pint whipped cream or whipped evaporated milk. Flavour to taste and freeze. This is improved by stirring well half-way through freezing time.

## QUICK ICE CREAM DESSERTS

Using tall glasses or goblets you can make a great variety of sundaes, which look as attractive as they taste.

*Pineapple Sundae:* Drain a tin of crushed pineapple, and place alternate spoonfuls of pineapple and ice cream into tall glasses, pushing the mixture well down in layers. Garnish each with a cherry.

*Chocolate Pear Sundae:* Well drained canned pear halves should be chopped into cubes and mixed with a little finely chopped crystallized ginger, then put alternate spoonfuls of chocolate ice cream and pears into tall glasses. Top with a spoonful of whipped cream and serve at once.

If no chocolate ice cream is available, grate some block chocolate and put alternate layers of ice cream, chocolate and chopped pears, finishing with whipped cream and a sprinkle of grated chocolate.

*Plumcake Sundae :* Cut rich fruit cake (stale if possible) into slices then crumble as small as possible. Sprinkle crumbs with a little sherry or orange juice, but do not make them too moist. Put alternate layers of cake crumbs and ice cream in glasses, pressing well down, then finish with a spoonful of whipped cream and garnish each with a cherry.

*Gingered Banana Sundae :* Crush gingernut biscuits into coarse crumbs. Peel several ripe bananas and mash with a fork, adding a little lemon juice to prevent discolouring. Put alternate layers of ice cream, gingernut crumbs and mashed banana into glasses, and finish with whipped cream and a sprinkle of crumbs on top.

*Quick Ice Cream Cake :* A single layer sponge cake makes a quick dessert when cut into two layers, spread with strawberry jam, then sandwiched together again with a thick layer of ice cream. Whip cream until thick and add a spoonful or two of strawberry jam, then spread over top of cake. Serve at once.

*Chocolate Ice Cream Cake :* Once in an emergency I brought home a round chocolate cream cake from our local cake shop, separated it into two layers, then sandwiched it together again with a thick layer of chocolate ice cream I had in the 'fridge. I then spread a thick layer of cream over the chocolate icing on top of the cake, and sprinkled it with chopped walnuts (bought ready chopped). The whole thing was done in about 8 minutes, and put into the refrigerator to chill through while the first course was served for dinner. Everybody thought it was a wonderful sweet, and asked me for the recipe, so remember this idea next time you are caught in an emergency rush.

## CASSATA BOMBE

This is a recipe for those with a large freezing compartment in their refrigerator, as it is made in a 2½-pint basin and will make 10 to 12 serves. If you prefer, the mixture can be halved and made in a bar-cake tin, putting alternate layers of the ice cream, cake mixture and cream mixture, finishing with a layer of ice cream. It can be made two or three days before serving as long as it is kept frozen and not thawed during that period.

1 *pint chocolate ice cream*
1 *pint vanilla ice cream*
½ *cup cake crumbs*
1 *tablespoon sherry or cherry brandy*
2 *tablespoons redcurrant or apple jelly*
*few drops red food colouring if necessary*

¼ *pint double cream*
4 *glacé cherries, chopped*
6 *blanched almonds, slivered*
1 *tablespoon castor sugar*
3 *teaspoons chopped peel*
*few drops almond essence*
1 *tablespoon coarsely grated chocolate*

Soften chocolate ice cream slightly and spread round the base and sides of a 2½-pint mould. Freeze until firm. Soften vanilla ice cream and spread in a layer over chocolate ice cream, leaving a hollow in the middle. Mix together the cake crumbs, redcurrant or apple jelly, cherry brandy or sherry, and food colouring to get a good colour, making sure they are well blended. Spoon into hollow in ice cream and chill until set.

Whip the cream with the sugar until thick, then fold in

remainder of ingredients. Spoon into hollow in basin on top of cake mixture and smooth over level with top of ice cream. These amounts should just fill basin, which should then be lightly covered with a piece of greaseproof paper cut to fit, or use a round of foil. Freeze bombe until firm, at least overnight.

When ready to serve, unmould by dipping basin into warm water for only a few seconds, then turn out on a serving plate. Replace in refrigerator until ready to bring to table. To serve, cut in wedges with a sharp knife. Whipped cream can be served with this, but it is not necessary.

## BRAZILIAN PARFAIT

The combination of coffee, chocolate and rum allied to vanilla ice cream makes this a most interesting frozen pudding. It can be frozen in refrigerator trays, or put into a mould and frozen like a bombe. It is then turned out and garnished with whipped cream and half walnuts.

| | |
|---|---|
| 1 *quart vanilla ice cream* | 2 *or 3 tablespoons rum* |
| 2 *teaspoons instant powdered* | *whipped cream* |
| *coffee* | *half walnuts* |
| 2 *tablespoons grated chocolate* | |

Mix coffee and rum together until dissolved. Break up the ice cream roughly and put spoonfuls into mould or tray alternately with the coffee-rum mixture and grated chocolate to give a marbled effect. Freeze until required. Turn out and serve with cream, and garnish with walnuts.

## ORANGE AND LEMON WATER ICE

After a rich and substantial dinner, a water ice makes a light and delicious finish to a good meal. Make it the night before and freeze until ready to serve next day, but do not keep it more than 2 days.

¾ *lb sugar*
1½ *pints water*
¾ *pint orange juice*

¼ *pint lemon juice*
*finely grated rind 1 orange and*
1 *lemon*

Boil sugar and water together for 5 minutes. Cool slightly and add orange and lemon juice and grated rind. Stir well and cool. When cold, strain through a fine sieve, pour into freezing trays and freeze until firm.

## PEACHES AND CREAM SHERBET

A very simply made frozen dessert, which is even simpler to make if you have an electric blender.

Drain a large can of peaches, and put peaches into the blender until smooth. If you haven't a blender, mash the drained peaches with a fork. Measure 2 cupfuls of peach pulp, and fold lightly into ½ pint stiffly whipped cream, sweetened to taste. Freeze until firm.

# Index